Canoe Camping
Vermont
&
New Hampshire Rivers

Canoe Camping
Vermont
&
New Hampshire Rivers

A Guide to 600 Miles of Rivers for a Day,
Weekend, or Week of Canoe Camping

Third Edition

Roioli Schweiker

Backcountry Guides
Woodstock, Vermont

An invitation to the reader

Rivers are notorious for changing course. Dams wash out, storms and floods re-arrange rocks, and new bridges and roads alter access points. If you run these rivers and find they have changed since this edition went to press, the author and publisher would appreciate hearing your corrections for future editions. And if you have suggestions for other rivers—or new books—we would like to hear those, too. Address all correspondence to: Editor, Backcountry Guides, PO Box 748, Woodstock, VT 05091

© 1977, 1985, 1989, 1999 by Roioli Schweiker
Third Edition

Library of Congress Cataloging in Publication Data
Schweiker, Roioli.
     Canoe camping Vermont & New Hampshire rivers : a guide to 600 miles of rivers for a day, weekend, or week of canoe camping / Roioli Schweiker. —3rd ed.
          p.   cm.
     Includes index.
     ISBN 0-88150-457-2 (paper)
     1. Canoes and canoeing—Vermont—Guidebooks. 2. Canoe camping—Vermont—Guidebooks. 3. Rivers—Vermont—Recreational use—Guidebooks. 4. Canoes and canoeing—New Hampshire—Guidebooks. 5. Canoe camping—New Hampshire—Guidebooks. 6. Rivers—New Hampshire—Recreational use—Guidebooks. I. Title. II. Title: Canoe camping Vermont and New Hampshire rivers.
GV776.V5S38 1999
917.4304'43—dc21   98-43779

Cover design by Joanna Bodenweber
Cover photograph by Rachel Cogbill
Text design by Faith Hague
Interior photographs by the author unless credited otherwise
Published by Backcountry Guides
A Division of The Countryman Press, Woodstock, Vermont 05091
Distributed by W. W. Norton, 500 Fifth Avenue, New York, New York 10110
Printed in the United States of America
10 9 8 7 6 5 4 3 2

Acknowledgments

In appreciation to all those who helped make this book possible:

The people who allowed me to load canoes, park, or camp on their property.

The people who helped me take new pictures by holding the canoe "right here," posing "just one more time," or reviewing rivers they know well: Mike Jacobs, Nancy Hoolihan, Tony Bogacki, Faith Knapp, Dick and Verniel Morin, Bob Gruber, Marjorie Walker, Al and Mary Batchelder, Peter Richardson, Mike Lebwohl, Joan Zardus, Irene Leavitt, Joe Correia, Elizabeth, Rick, and Alice Burt, Debra Clark, Gene Daniell, and Alexander Cogbill.

Rachel Walker Cogbill, the only person who was able to help on all three editions. She also took the original author photo on the first two editions, and the cover photo for this edition.

Of course my husband, Robert; my son, Roy; my daughter, Viloya.

Roioli Schweiker

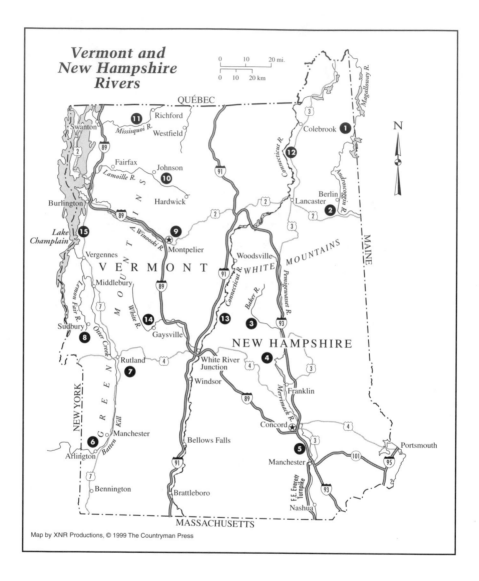

Vermont and New Hampshire Rivers

QUÉBEC

0   10   20 mi.
0   10   20 km

Richford

Swanton   *Missisquoi R.*   Westfield

Colebrook **❶**

⓫

⓬

Fairfax   Johnson

Lamoille R.   **❿**

Berlin

Lancaster   **❷**

Burlington

Hardwick

Andoscoggin R.

MAINE

Connecticut R.

Magalloway R.

Lake
Champlain **⓯**

Winooski R.

☆ Montpelier

Woodsville

WHITE MOUNTAINS

Vergennes

V E R M O N T

Middlebury

Connecticut R.

Baker R.

Pemigewasset R.

White R.   **⓭**

❸

93

Sudbury   **⓮**

Gaysville

NEW HAMPSHIRE

❽

Otter Creek

Rutland   **❼**

White River
Junction

Windsor

Franklin

❹

Merrimack R.

Concord ☆

G R E E N

Manchester   **❻**

Batten Kill

Arlington

Bellows Falls

Manchester   **❺**

Portsmouth

95

101

Bennington

Brattleboro

F.E. Everett
Turnpike

93

Nashua

MASSACHUSETTS

NEW YORK

MOUNTAINS

Vermont Fair R.

N

Map by XNR Productions, © 1999 The Countryman Press

Contents

Introduction. 9

Comments on the Third Edition 9

General Information. 10

Using the River Descriptions 23

1. Magalloway River–Umbagog Lake. 33

2. Androscoggin River 39

3. Baker River 45

4. Pemigewasset River 51

5. Merrimack River 59

6. Batten Kill. 69

7. Otter Creek 75

8. Lemon Fair River–Otter Creek 81

9. Winooski River 87

10. Lamoille River 95

11. Missisquoi River 103

12. Connecticut River (West Stewartstown to Gilman) 113

13. Connecticut River (Comerford Dam to Orford). 123

14. White River–Connecticut River 131

15. Lake Champlain. 141

Introduction

Comments on the Third Edition

For this new edition, fresh pictures were needed and rivers had to be rechecked. For the first half of the canoeing season the operative word was *water:* overhead and in the rivers. Many trips were canceled or postponed because the rivers were in flood; photography was impossible.

The high water of the past few years has greatly increased the problem of fallen trees. Some completely blocked the smaller rivers where they never had before, such as the upper Missisquoi. Others became dangerous sweepers on the outside curves of larger rivers. Some have been removed by river cleanup projects; others will take longer to disappear.

Several dams and power stations have been rebuilt, making the carry longer; often it is no longer possible to drive all the way to the river. The roads that must be crossed are much busier, and in some cases dangerous places to hand-carry a canoe.

Kayaks of all kinds are proliferating, from the sea kayaks used on large bodies of water to the all-purpose kind seen everywhere. These small plastic kayaks are handy, lightweight to carry or drag, easier to learn to use than a canoe, and suitable for small lakes and easy rivers.

The number of canoe liveries has increased. Many of these rivers now have available a boat and shuttle service for day trips. A few offer inn-to-inn paddling.

Canoe trails are becoming established in several places, with the goal of having campsites available a day's paddle apart. Many of these are maintained by volunteer work parties. Your help is appreciated to work on these campsites, or to keep them neat when you use them.

Canoeing is a wonderful activity suitable for a wide age range. There was a 78-year age spread among the people who helped me on this revision, from 5 to 83; the two extremes each camped for at least two consecutive nights with me. We all had a wonderful time; well, most of the time, anyway.

Your comments and corrections are requested. However, please remember that even if I am aware of a change, it will not magically alter the text of books already printed!

Many of you have recognized me along the river, and I look forward to seeing many more of you there in the future.

General Information

The canoe trips described here introduce you to some lesser-known Vermont and New Hampshire rivers as well as a few more popular runs. A chief attraction of these rivers is their accessibility. All are convenient to numbered highways, making arrival and car shuttling relatively simple, and numerous bridges and launching spots offer a fair degree of flexibility. The many access points allow you to run these rivers as a series of day trips or short camping trips, and none has quotas or requires advance registration. You need only obtain permission to cross or use privately owned property.

The river trips are arranged by watershed and run from just under 20 miles to almost 80 miles. All offer a weekend or more of leisurely family canoeing and generally have enough water to be run for some of their length throughout the usual canoe camping season (mid-May to early autumn).

No trip is extremely demanding, but the descriptions assume basic canoeing knowledge and some experience in selecting rivers and landing spots above ledges and dams. Those less skilled should use caution and inspect all trouble spots in advance from the shore. This guide does not explain how to canoe; it does describe places to canoe and tells you what to expect from each river.

In other respects these rivers differ considerably. Some flow through sparsely settled woodlands, others across rolling farmland, and a few through cities. Some are entirely flatwater; others have rapids of varying length and difficulty. Two consist almost entirely of rapids. Although only a few big rapids have heavy water during the summer, experienced canoeists should find the lower water on these trips as challenging in its own way as roaring rapids. While warmer water and weather reduce danger, shallow water calls for greater skill in reading water and maneuvering a canoe.

Along with river descriptions I have included directions for short hikes near the riverbanks and notes on swimming holes, campsites, picnic areas, and historical sites that should help you choose a river suited to your particular interests.

Safety

No guidebook can substitute for canoeing skill and alertness. If you cannot stop in the distance you can see ahead, you are canoeing beyond your ability. It is possible to stop anywhere within a canoe length or two—even in the middle of a rapid—if you know how. Novice paddlers should consult books that explain techniques of setting (bow downstream) and ferrying (bow upstream)—techniques that enable you to paddle directly across a fast current among rocks so that you do not get swept farther downstream. Always make practice runs on familiar rivers, preferably with a group that has rescue potential.

Keep your canoe under control. When landing in a fast current, your upstream end should always touch in to shore first. Approach sharp river bends cautiously on the inside, again with the stern well in toward shore for easy landing in case any obstacles, such as fallen trees, should suddenly appear.

Federal laws require a personal flotation device (PFD) for each person on board. Serious canoeists wear a comfortable life jacket whenever running rapids, canoeing lakes in a wind, or wearing encumbering clothing (rain suits, rubber boots). Poor swimmers should always wear life jackets, and nonswimmers should not canoe on fast-moving rivers at all. Test your PFDs occasionally to check their flotation: The filler loses its buoyancy with age, and even faster if the devices are used as cushions. PFDs for small children should have crotch straps, especially those that are bought large "to grow into." If you are wearing one at all, the straps should be tight, or it may come off when you need it most.

If I could pick only one rule for canoe safety it would be: *Don't paddle any river you are not willing to swim.*

Hazards

Next to PWI (paddling while intoxicated), the chief cause of serious canoeing accidents is getting entangled in fallen trees. Their location cannot be documented, because conditions may change overnight. They are usually located around blind corners where the current sweeps the canoe into them and are especially hazardous in high water. Bridge pilings also collect debris; avoid paddling too soon after a flood, when the water is full of debris.

While trees may produce the same sort of hydraulics (turbulent conditions) as rocks or other obstacles, they are also likely to have water flowing *under* them, with submerged branches that prevent free passage of objects.

Picture the following scenario: The trunk of the tree is just above water level. A canoe strikes it and swings broadside. The current sucks the upstream gunwale under, and the paddlers wash under the boat, where tree branches keep them from surfacing. The only protection is to canoe conservatively and under control at all times.

Dams are a particular hazard. The current often speeds up just before them, and retaining walls or steep banks may also confine the river. Dam gates open and close in seemingly arbitrary fashion, and the water level in the river below may quickly rise or fall as much as several feet. Most people recognize the dangers in a high dam or steep drop, but the backroller of a fairly low dam or ledge can sometimes trap a canoe—and canoeist—where they may churn around in the froth indefinitely.

Blackflies are usually at their peak for a couple of weeks during June, while mosquitoes are active throughout the summer. Defenses against insects range from wearing a head net and gloves along with clothing that has zippers and elastic instead of buttons, to applying a wide selection of sprays and ointments, to simply staying home during the worst of the bug season. In summer camping a bugproof tent is a must for all but the most repellent old woodsman.

Learn to recognize and avoid poison ivy; unfortunately, this plant favors sunny riverbanks. A good wash soon after exposure, even in cold water, will help. The oil remains on clothing and shoes, so wash them, too.

A tan you may have already acquired is no protection against a full day of exposure to the sun's powerful rays reflecting off the water. Reflected sunlight can burn you even on cloudy days, so take cover-up clothing and sun hats, and put them on before it's too late. A sunscreen with a high SPF helps, but it is no substitute for clothing. It is possible to get a burn even through a lightweight shirt! More summer trips are spoiled by an overdose of sun than by anything else. Sunglasses reduce glare reflected off the water.

Clothing

Many people like to canoe in a bathing suit; this is fine for a while, but be sure to take along more protective clothing—a hat, a long-sleeved shirt, long pants, socks, and gloves.

Snowfall is not uncommon as late as May, and even summers are often cold enough to warrant paddling in warm slacks and shirts. Carry a spare set of dry clothing in case of an accident or a sudden drop in temperature; woolens and the new synthetic fabrics are recommended: They dry quickly and are warm when wet. Additional warm clothing frequently makes the difference between continuing a trip and going home. Blue jeans and cotton sweatshirts are the worst possible choice for canoeing; they hold water like a sponge, are chilly when wet, and take forever to dry.

Wading shoes should be worn, particularly on rivers with rapids. Swim shoes or athletic shoes are usually sufficient against sharp stones and broken glass, but someone lining or wrestling with a loaded canoe in shallow rapids might prefer more protection.

A rain suit is the best protection the canoeist has against the weather. The plastic kind usually do not last even one trip; while the heavy-duty cloth backed models are more expensive, their durability makes the difference worthwhile. Ponchos dangerously hamper your swimming ability and also get in the way of paddling.

Equipment

The equipment you choose for a canoe camping trip should reflect your own taste and budget along with the type of trip planned. Basic gear includes a canoe, paddles, lines, waterproof packs, and an emergency kit. If you need more information on canoe camping gear, consult books on the subject or talk with experienced canoeists and reputable canoe stores. Beginners can find several canoe outfitters in northern New England who will rent all the equipment necessary for a comfortable trip. Names of rental outfitters can be obtained from local chambers of commerce, advertisements in canoeing magazines, or the Yellow Pages.

While almost any type of canoe will do for canoe camping, one 15 to 17 feet long is best for the rivers in this book. Canoes of this length are large enough to carry a reasonable load yet easy to handle and portage. Flatwater kayaks are popular these days, and can carry a small load.

A third paddle provides a spare for emergencies and is handy if you use paddles of different lengths for smooth water and for rapids.

Attach a 15-foot painter (rope), ⅜ inch in diameter, to each end of your canoe. These lines are useful for tying up, lining past rapids, and hauling up steep banks; if worse comes to worst, they are also a great help in rescuing a

Bowline with half hitches on a bight

swamped canoe. Nylon resists abrasion, but some people like the plastic lines that float. If you paddle a lot, marine line from a boating store may be worth buying. Smaller lines may be strong enough but they are hard to grip with a cold, wet hand and tend to kink up and knot. In any case, use rope with a stiff lay that will not tangle around your feet.

Waterproofing essential equipment is a bit of a nuisance but worth the effort. All kinds of waterproof packs are available at sporting goods stores, but some advertised as waterproof are only water repellent. *Test* them in advance, particularly the seal. Most of them work well when new, but many become less effective as they get older. Before purchasing any waterproof pack, consider how easy it is to open and close, to portage, and to tie into a canoe. If you can find them, old army ammunition boxes come in a variety of sizes and make excellent waterproof packing for small items and cameras. So do the large institutional-size plastic jars for foods like pickles and mayonnaise; you might try to obtain some of these from your neighborhood restaurant or school lunch program. Friction tops tend to pop off under stress, so use screw-top containers. Sometimes you need an extra liner in the lid to make the container waterproof; you can cut one from a water-resistant food package. Dive boxes are also good. Plastic garbage bags are too flimsy to offer useful protection.

Canteens, cooking pots, sunscreen, combs, and such do not need to be packed waterproof. And remember that containers full of liquid have been known to leak all over your dry stuff.

Making a Waterproof Bag

Waterproof bags for packing clothing, bedding, and foodstuffs are easy and inexpensive to make from heavy-duty plastic. You can find this sold by the yard in fabric stores and hardware stores, and on the display with plastic tablecloth material. It is 45 inches wide and comes in four weights; one of the middle weights is best.

Cut the material into a rectangle twice the size of the finished bag plus 2 inches each way (45 x 36 inches works nicely). Fold the material as for a pillowcase. Seal two edges by protecting with waxed paper and running an iron on medium-low heat along them for four or five seconds (test first on a scrap: practice making a small bag for a purse or map). Also test the bag in case there is an airhole. Seal the bag by folding the top over several times after pressing the air out. The seal is better if it is folded over a thin piece of wood, or even cardboard. Fasten with clips; binder clips work well. To keep track of the clips, put a piece of duct tape on the side of the bag, punch a hole, tie the clips on spaced out, and tie the end of the cord to the hole in the duct tape. To close the bag properly, do not pack it more than two-thirds full. Put this bag inside a cloth bag to carry and tie into the boat.

A bag may be made to fit an item of any size, such as a map or

ROY SCHWEIKER

Rolling and sealing the top of a plastic waterproof bag with clips.

wallet, or custom-fitted to any size or shape of container you have. Be sure to leave enough spare material to seal.

Tents

The vast majority of tents seem to be poorly designed—they are intended to be put up and taken down in good weather. How many publicity pictures have you seen of someone getting into a tent in the pouring rain? Yet this is when you really need one! Most of the dome tents let in vast quantities of water during entry, soaking your clothing and equipment.

A plastic tarp over the tent will give you a "porch" for stowing wet boots and ponchos, as well as ensuring a dry entry. Since the tarp stands separately, the tent may be erected or taken down dry underneath it. We sometimes put the tarp up, cook dinner on a stove underneath it, and then erect the tent; with a larger porch you can cook in front of the tent.

NANCY HOOLIHAN

Packing up on a wet morning on the "porch" of the tent. Note the use of the canoe paddle for a tarp pole.

I cut a suitable size from 10 x 25-foot plastic tarps, which come in 3 or 4 ml thickness. The corners and other tie points should be reinforced with duct tape and the hole punched. I use canoe paddles for end poles, because they add very little weight.

Tarps must be replaced occasionally. Still, the only two times I have had trouble with wind has been when conditions involved major damage to other structures.

Packing

All your equipment, except possibly a rock collection or a sack of canned goods that can be jettisoned, should be tied into the canoe so it will not slide around or be lost in a spill. The school of thought that suggests not tying in your gear has little to recommend it. Should you swamp or capsize, only a very efficient rescue squad could salvage loose gear before it floats off. Furthermore, a properly waterproofed duffel bag floats high in the water; tied in a swamped canoe, it will improve the canoe's balance and increase its buoyancy. To tie in your gear, use a light rope that can be cut easily should the canoe be pinned.

Have a pack of some kind to carry small items to use while underway, and to contain clothing, hats, sunglasses, and other items you may want to take on and off during the trip. Your small packet of emergency items should include a first-aid kit and a roll of duct tape. The tape is indispensable for patching holes in canoes, rain suits, and other items. If applied to a dry surface, it continues to hold after it gets wet. A small sewing kit, complete with thread, needles, pins, buttons, extra cloth, and folding scissors, is very handy. Also take along a knife, a small tube of waterproof glue, extra cord, waterproof matches, and a compass. *Note:* Waterproof safety matches are useless unless packed waterproof, because the striking surface is dissolved by water!

Car keys going missing is sometimes a serious problem. I strongly feel that you should hide a key on the outside of each car. Car thieves will put a rock through the window (discourage this by not leaving valuables in the car) or punch out the ignition; the only people inconvenienced by the lack of a hidden key are yourself and your companions. Get duplicates of your house and car keys and leave the huge ring behind.

Put your name on any equipment you care about; this facilitates its return. Also, some of us are getting tired of playing King Solomon when not all of the identical equipment makes it to the end.

Canoes packed low to improve handling and reduce wind resistance.

Loading the Canoe

The canoe should be loaded with good trim (distribution of weight) both back to front and sideways, taking into account the weight of the paddlers. Put camping equipment on the bottom, and things you will need during the day—like day packs and the lunch bag—where they are easy to reach. As food is used up, the packing plan may be altered. Everything should be packed level with the gunwales or below, if possible, to keep the weight low and to offer less wind resistance.

Everything should be tied in, the manner depending on the difficulty of the trip. Waterproof bags of clothing and sleeping bags offer a great deal of flotation to a swamped canoe, and should be tied in so as to make the most of this where needed. Sometimes sticks are placed on the floor of the canoe under the duffel to allow the water to drain back to the end for bailing.

Unless you have a large party, load the canoe in the water to avoid being stranded high and dry!

Portaging

For a short portage it may be easier for four to eight people to pick up the loaded canoe and carry it around without unloading.

If portages are a feature of the trip, though, pack your gear in parcels that keep it together and are easy to carry. Items light enough to carry in one hand should have a handle or rope so they can be carried that way. Larger items such as coolers are more conveniently carried by two people. On a narrow trail, walk in single file.

Where there is a great deal of loose lightweight gear, it may be easier to carry the canoe right-side up and keep it all together.

Count how many parcels, and what kind, you have in the canoe. Re-count them when you reach the end of the portage to make sure you have everything. Pile all gear from the canoe in a single pile at each end. If a group is carrying each other's gear, pile it all in one big pile. Then after every one has claimed their gear, leftover items will be obvious and will not get left behind.

Canoeing with Children

Properly introduced to it, children enjoy a canoe camping trip as much as adults. Children should not canoe camp on rivers with white water until age 11 or 12, or when old enough to paddle well and swim with confidence. They must have confidence that they can stay afloat and get to shore under various conditions. Children should learn to swim in fast water and waves— it is essential practice for a spill in the rapids. Another way to maintain

A canoe wash is fun swimming practice for youngsters.

interest is to get children their own equipment. Young children find regular paddles, especially those for white-water, too cumbersome to manage. My daughter had her own red paddle with a special design and her name on it, to which she long had a sentimental attachment. Do not force your children to paddle. Children should also have their own properly fitting life jacket and rain gear.

On flatwater trips you might bring nature books to help identify wildlife and geologic structures. Plan time for children to explore the woods, swim, or fish. Fun projects like a canoe wash increase confidence: Take the canoe out in deep water, roll it over and back, wash the inside, and roll over again several times. On some muddy rivers I was overjoyed to volunteer my canoe for this.

Camping

Private campgrounds, some catering to canoeists, front a few of these rivers and are mentioned in the text. I have not attempted to name each one separately, since campgrounds, like rental outfitters, come and go. Current listings of all New Hampshire and Vermont campgrounds are available from government agencies in each state. Local chambers of commerce also offer lists of campgrounds in their area.

Many of these rivers, however, have few or no campgrounds along their banks, so you must make your own arrangements in advance with individual property owners. Most flow through farmland for some of their distance, and if approached properly many farmers do allow canoeists to camp on their property. Send the most personable member of your party, suitably dressed, for best results.

If permission to camp is refused, be courteous and understanding, and leave; if it is granted, be considerate, quiet, and unobtrusive. Take your litter and trash with you, be careful, use low-impact camping techniques, and if you have permission for a fire, don't leave messy, charred remains. Remember that farmers depend on their fields and pastures for their livelihood—leave gates as you find them and walk along the fence lines rather than across the fields. The granting of permission to canoeists who follow you is determined by your behavior.

Some new campsites have been opened along the rivers, but many others have been closed by owners who have withdrawn permission to camp in areas that we formerly used because of inconsiderate campers.

Tubing

The use of inner tubes, air mattresses, and other floating objects has seen a great upsurge in popularity. They have the advantage of being cheap, portable, and available, and some places even rent them. Tubing is fun, but it is also dangerous. Tubers have little visibility ahead and (like many canoeists) often don't know the proper way to control their craft. Many have drowned by being swept under trees or over falls. Note that many people canoeing on these same stretches of river will be wearing life jackets!

If you are a beginner at tubing, select a stretch of river that you know—either from other people or from visual inspection—to be free of hazards. Choose a sunny day with the temperature well above 70 degrees. Plan on a maximum of an hour afloat, and allow for time to get out of the water and warm up along the way. Mountain streams are still very cold even in the summer.

We often carry tubes on our canoe trips, and at an interesting stretch of rapids we don't carry the canoe back and rerun them, we carry the tubes back instead. The tubes also give our canoes extra flotation in the rapids and serve as "beanbag" chairs around camp.

Hiking

Several hiking trails adjoin these rivers. The Long Trail, Vermont's Green Mountain footpath, crosses the Winooski and the Lamoille along the portions described here, and the Appalachian Trail crosses the White River at West Hartford. Directions for short hikes along these and other paths and roads that lead to particularly interesting summits, gorges, or ponds are given in the individual river sections.

Maps

The best all-around maps for out purposes can be found in the *Vermont Atlas and Gazetteer* and *New Hampshire Atlas and Gazetteer,* which each contain topographic maps of the entire state. They can be found in most local bookstores and sporting goods stores, or ordered directly from the publisher:

DeLorme
PO Box 298
Yarmouth, Maine 04096
207-846-7000

Addresses

Current listings of campgrounds (in New Hampshire, called *New Hampshire Camping Guide*) and excellent state highway maps (which also list historical sites and state parks) are available from:

Division of Economic Development
PO Box 1856
Concord, NH 03302
603-271-3627
e-mail: nhparks@dred.state.nh.us
or
Vermont Department of Forests, Parks & Recreation
103 South Main Street
Waterbury, VT 05671-0603
802-241-3655

For information regarding fishing conditions and regulations, contact the following:

New Hampshire Fish and Game Department
Hazen Drive
Concord, NH 03302
603-271-3422
or
Vermont Fish and Wildlife Department
103 South Main Street
Waterbury, VT 05671-0501
802-241-3700

For information on Vermont's Long Trail:

Long Trail Guide
c/o Green Mountain Club
RR1, Box 650, Route 100
Waterbury Center, VT 05677
802-244-7037
web site: www.greenmountainclub.org/index.cfm

The Appalachian Mountain Club promotes canoeing and hiking throughout New England; lists of local canoe chapters and other information can be obtained from:

Appalachian Mountain Club
5 Joy Street
Boston, MA 02108
617-523-0655
web site: www.outdoors.org/

Using the River Descriptions

Each canoe trip includes maps, a brief introduction to the river, a summary table, and detailed descriptions of each river segment.

The maps in this book are intended for use in conjunction with a good highway map as well as other more detailed maps, if desired. The approximate scale is the same for all the maps: 1 inch to 3 miles. North is at the top of the map. The following symbols are standard:

river	path
road	covered bridge
launching ramp	campsite
railroad	

A good highway map should get you to your starting point and provide a general picture of the river's course and the terrain through which it flows. You can get these maps from state tourist bureaus, gas stations, or bookstores.

The maps that accompany the descriptions were drawn specifically for this guidebook and show the breakpoints (where a section of river description ends and another one begins); hazardous obstructions, difficult rapids, bridges, nearby roads, and hiking trails mentioned in the text.

Each river has been broken down into short sections. Where feasible, each segment contains water conditions of similar difficulty. In some instances breakpoints occur at the most likely spot to end or begin a trip (such as dams). In many cases, these segments also make good day trips, but they were not specifically chosen for that reason.

"Right bank" and "left bank" as used in the text always refer to your position as if you are in the river facing downstream, regardless of your actual orientation.

I have not attempted to give a foot-by-foot description of each river.

Rather, this guide should provide a general description of the type of canoeing you can expect on each river as well as the locations of all the more difficult spots. *Note:* Rivers often change abruptly, so use caution, and always have your canoe under control.

I cannot provide meaningful estimates for the time needed to cover the rivers. Everybody paddles at a different rate, the current speed changes with different water levels, and the wind may be either with you or against you. Furthermore, people stop at different times to watch birds, pick flowers and berries, examine rocks, swim, fish, take photographs, hike, and recover from accidents. In general, it takes a large group longer to cover a given distance than a small one.

Remember to leave time for necessary car shuttles. These can be big time wasters, particularly if they are poorly organized. Good logistics can greatly increase the time you have available for canoeing.

I also have not attempted to rate the scenery. Some people want nothing but wilderness, while others prefer their riverbanks studded with white church steeples and old mills. Civil engineers like bridges, and gardening enthusiasts inspect the crops.

Summary Tables

Each river trip is accompanied by a summary chart. Cumulative mileages to the left of the breakpoints refer to the total distance from the start to the breakpoints; the ratings and special difficulties noted on the right refer to those sections of the river that run between two break points.

Mileages. The mileages given in the chart and in each river description were usually measured from the 15-minute USGS topographic maps to the nearest ¼ mile. Cumulative distances were measured from an arbitrary starting point and cover the entire river segment, including parts that must be portaged. These figures also appear in parenthesis throughout the text as reference points.

River Rating. Throughout this book, I have used the international whitewater rating scale to describe the relative difficulty of each stretch of the river. Although elaborate charts tell you how to compute river ratings, any classification remains essentially subjective:

F: Flatwater. The canoe will not drift noticeably with the current. Upstream paddling is easy. Minor obstacles can be easily avoided.

Fallen trees frequently block small streams after a storm.

Q: Quickwater. The current is strong enough to make paddling upstream difficult. Obstacles can be avoided by careful application of flatwater canoeing techniques.

1: Easy rapids. White-water canoeing skills are useful. Rapids may have shallow riffles with only one clear channel, or waves that can be run nearly anywhere. Rocks or fallen trees may require dodging in a slow current. Spilled boats can usually be recovered without severe difficulty.

2: Medium rapids. White-water canoeing skills are essential. Rapids have waves and/or require rock dodging in a fast current. Ledges have few clear channels. Rescue of spilled boats and boaters may be difficult.

3: Difficult rapids. These should be run only by experienced white-water canoeists. Rapids and ledges have intricate routes, large waves, turbulence, and hydraulics (places where the water churns around back upstream and can hold a boat or person indefinitely). Boats may be smashed, pinned so rescue is difficult, or washed downstream. Serious injury to boaters is possible.

Special Difficulties. The chart notes difficulties in excess of the rating assigned to that section, so read the rating column carefully. A section rated 2 does not have any class 2 or even easy class 3 rapids listed under "Special Difficulties," while a class 1 rapid does receive special attention in a section rated F.

An obstruction marked with an asterisk occurs at the breakpoint and therefore does not require an additional portage for those who start or end a trip at that point.

Fallen trees shift with every rainstorm and often wash great distances downstream, so they can turn up almost anywhere. Only rivers that customarily have extensive fallen trees in a specific area receive special attention in the chart.

Reading Water

The classic instruction for running white water is to head for the longest "V" on the theory that since the upstream point of the "V" is a rock, the longest downstream "V" gives the greatest space between the rocks. This works well when the river is straight and the rocks few. But the river is often not straight, the current whipping from one side to another like a drunken snake. This means the current is seldom parallel to the bank—a feature that is often overlooked.

The fastest and deepest current is on the outside of the curves, as well as the biggest waves and most of the fallen trees. The slower current is on the inside, but the shallowest water is also found here, and often there is no clear channel through. The best strategy may be to paddle on either side, crossing back and forth, or perhaps taking the middle, depending on the height of the water and the speed of the current, as well as the obstacles present.

Water Level

The water level depends on the amount of rainfall and varies so much from day to day that it is not possible to predict exactly when a river can be run. Furthermore, the canoeist's water-reading skill is more important than a gauge reading in determining the minimum water level required. Experts at handling a boat and reading water can take a loaded canoe down a stretch that others may consider totally unrunnable; this greatly increases the mileage of rivers available for canoeing.

When you are deciding whether the river has enough water to run remember that the water is usually deeper than it appears from the shore.

Determining River Conditions

		STREAM CHARACTERISTICS			
		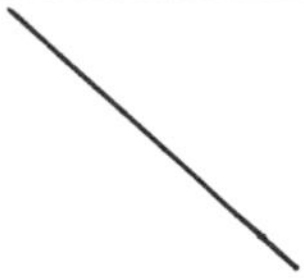	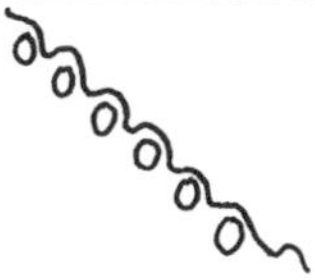		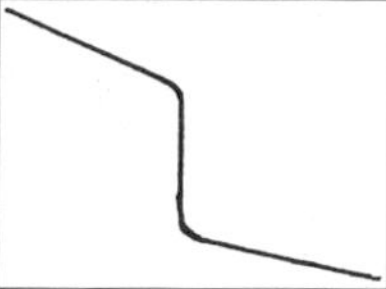
		Even gradient; sandy or gravel bottom	Even gradient; larger wastebasket-sized rocks	Drop in chutes around table-sized rocks	Smooth water with ledges or dams
WATER LEVEL	Low Water	Runnable; occasional wading over bars	Unrunnable; just wet rocks	Often one deep channel that can be run with occasional lining	Flatwater; line or portage drops
	Medium Water	Class 1 run	Class 2 run	Class 2 run	Quickwater and portage
	High Water	Washes out to only a fast current	Washes out to series of waves	Big waves and eddies (class 3)	Chance of being swept over drop; portage greatly lengthened

Also, the old poling technique is becoming popular again in shallow rivers and when going upstream.

In general, the faster upper reaches of these rivers require higher water to run than the slower lower reaches, and rapids demand more water than flat stretches. A few sections must be run in medium water, usually found only in May or after rainstorms. All but two rivers in this guidebook can be run throughout an ordinarily wet summer. The water levels of some are totally controlled by dams.

Canoeists have a variety of choices that depend on water conditions. If the lower river is high and muddy, run a stretch farther upstream; when the

Packing up after breakfast. We take our canoes to higher ground at night for safekeeping.

upper parts are too shallow, the flat, lower sections are still available.

The diagram on page 27 indicates the effect different water levels have on different types of riverbeds. In each example, the river drops an average of 15 feet per mile.

Access

Good access points are generally mentioned in the text. In theory, any bridge can provide access along the highway right-of-way. In actuality, some are very high with poor footing or have no shoulder for parking and loading or unloading canoes. Access may be possible where the river comes to the road, but the banks are frequently steep and overgrown. Power companies and public agencies have provided accesses to some rivers.

Many access points cross private land; in such cases, ask the owners' permission before using them. Obey any specific instructions, and be careful to leave your car where it will not block gates or other cars. Be considerate; a landowner's feelings reflect the behavior of the last group that used his property, and you may have to spend some time searching around and asking permission in advance.

Unfortunately, some take-outs above dams are very difficult, especially in high water. Where access is necessary (for example, by dams) but none is recommended, it is because I could not find a spot worth recommending. In time perhaps, things may change and you might do better.

Launching the Canoe

Many pictures show the canoe being launched bow-first from a sand beach. However, launching the canoe stern-first has many advantages. It is easier to step into the canoe in the bow. It requires a long leg to step in front of the stern seat. Stepping in the small space behind it, where it is even possible, is unstable, and loss of balance may result in a wrenched leg or worse. Once the paddlers have sat down, the canoe may still be stuck on the shore, while the difference in weight placement with the bow toward shore means the canoe will usually float free, and can be turned around with draw strokes.

Launching the canoe stern first makes it easier to get in to.

In cases where the water is deep enough, the canoe may be pulled sideways to shore or dock and the paddlers can each step into the chosen end.

The Zorro Launch

Sometimes it is necessary to put the canoe in the water with the bow downstream, as when lifting over an obstruction, or from an awkward start in a rapid. The stern paddler may be teetering unhappily on unstable footing, grasping the point of the canoe wondering what to do next. A bold move will solve this problem! Lean forward and grasp the sides of the canoe as far forward as possible, with one hand on each side. Straddling the deck, push off, swing your feet up and into the canoe, and toboggan down the deck into the stern seat. The bow paddler should maintain control while this is going on.

Strokes

The majority of self-taught canoeists, and many who learned from a friend, think they are doing a J stroke when they are really doing a stern pry. While a stern pry is the stroke of choice in fast water, a J stroke is 50 percent faster in flat water, because the control does not slow the canoe down. It seems much more awkward at first, but is well worth learning to do right. It is best learned from a good paddler rather than from a book.

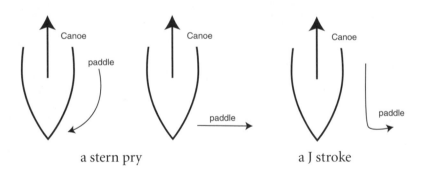

a stern pry   a J stroke

Scouting

Unless your group is very experienced and confident, inspect take-outs and difficult spots before starting the trip. When northern New England was first settled, drops in rivers were the only source of mechanical power. Saw- and gristmills were built next to dams at the drops, and frequently towns grew up around them. Bridge engineers had the same requirements as dam builders—a spot narrow enough for the crossing along with solid rock footings. The demand for bridges was greatest at towns; thus, almost all the rapids and old dams along these rivers are conveniently located underneath bridges in the middle of town. Newer dams have access roads to them.

This makes advance scouting of many difficult places relatively easy. While spotting cars, you can locate the most suitable place to portage, put in, and take out; and you can ask for necessary permission to cross private property. You can also decide whether to line or run a rapid and where to land if additional scouting should be necessary. Advance scouting also helps the river leader recognize from above the difficult spots that can be hard to visualize from printed instructions, and it can save a lot of walking down the bank. Directions for advance scouting from the road are given in the text.

1

Magalloway River–Umbagog Lake

Miles	Cumulative Miles	Breakpoints	River Rating	Special Difficulties
	0	Wilson's Mills, Maine		
16			F	
	16	Umbagog Lake		
3¾			F	
	19¾	Errol Landing		Dam*
* Does not require portage if taking out at breakpoint.				

Magalloway River

Remote but easily accessible, the Magalloway River lies north of the White Mountains along the sparsely settled Maine–New Hampshire border. Rising in the timbered hills of the northwestern corner of Maine, it flows southward through man-made Aziscohos Lake before turning southwest to cross the border into New Hampshire. Just east of Errol, it joins the Umbagog Lake outlets to form the Androscoggin River. Even the most experienced canoeist may find its upper reaches rough, but the lower portion, from Wilson's Mills in Maine to the Errol Dam in New Hampshire, makes an excellent run for a first canoe camping expedition. A side trip around Umbagog Lake, connected to the Magalloway by short, unimpeded channels, is a bonus.

Unlike many northern New England rivers, the Magalloway runs clean, wandering across vast woodland tracts dominated by spruce and fir. The river is placid below Wilson's Mills, and since the dams at Errol

33

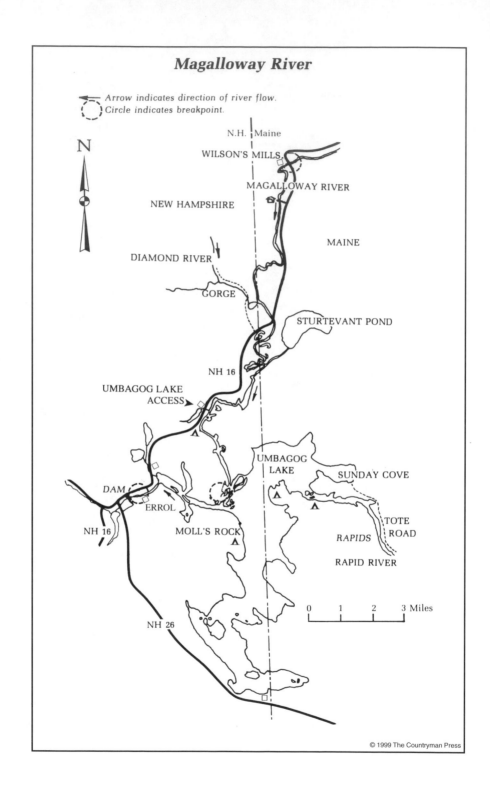

Magalloway River

Arrow indicates direction of river flow.
Circle indicates breakpoint.

N

N.H. Maine

WILSON'S MILLS

MAGALLOWAY RIVER

NEW HAMPSHIRE

MAINE

DIAMOND RIVER

GORGE

STURTEVANT POND

NH 16

UMBAGOG LAKE
ACCESS

UMBAGOG
LAKE

SUNDAY COVE

DAM

ERROL

MOLL'S ROCK

TOTE
ROAD

NH 16

RAPIDS

RAPID RIVER

NH 26

0   1   2   3 Miles

© 1999 The Countryman Press

and at Aziscohos Lake control water flow, the river can be canoed during the drier months.

A number of campsites have been established in the area. Many are accessible from the water. The campsites along the Magalloway River, as well as Mollidgewock Campground near NH 16, are administered by the state of New Hampshire (603-788-3155). The Cedar Stump Campsite at the mouth of the Rapid River is administered by Saco Bound (603-447-2177; the Errol site 603-482-3817). All campsites on Umbagog Lake are administered by Umbagog Lake Camps on NH 26 (603-482-7795). Reservations are required, and a fairly high use fee is charged.

Wilson's Mills to Umbagog Lake (16 miles)

To put in, drive north from Errol on NH 16 to the bridge at Wilson's Mills, Maine. The river contains difficult rapids upstream but flows smoothly below Wilson's Mills, meandering back and forth through swamps and oxbow lakes. Although the highway closely follows the river for much of the way, few houses or other evidence of modern civilization interrupt the pleasant illusion of a true wilderness region.

The Diamond River, which drains a Dartmouth College land grant, enters on the right 7 miles (mi. 7) from Wilson's Mills. The Diamond cuts through a spectacular gorge about 2 miles from its confluence with the Magalloway, and you may wish to make a short side trip here. A private gravel road just east of Wentworth Location on NH 16 will take you to a gate; cars are allowed beyond here only by permit from Dartmouth College, but pedestrians and cyclists are welcome. A 1-mile hike up the road carries you along the cliffs that line the gorge.

Nine miles (mi. 9) from Wilson's Mills, Sturtevant Pond Outlet flows into the Magalloway from the left. Some campsites in this vicinity are accessible by both car and canoe.

At mile 13 the river starts to swing away from the road in a big marsh-lined loop toward Umbagog Lake. (Just before this is the UMBAGOG LAKE ACCESS sign and a primitive launching ramp.) At the end of this 3-mile loop (mi. 16), a maze of side channels appears to the left. These waterways, which flow through marshes and past numerous small islands, are outlets from Umbagog Lake. In season, white pond lilies thrive in the shallow, slowly moving waters and in places are so thick they reduce the channels'

White water lilies frequently narrow the channel in shallow, marshy areas.

centers to a canoe's width or less and necessitate some pushing and poling.

In former times the Magalloway River and the outlet from Umbagog Lake met to form the Androscoggin River. Now the dam at Errol has raised the water level and flooded out the entire area, so it is hard to identify this point in the maze of channels.

Here, where the river becomes the Androscoggin, you have three choices: to return back up the Magalloway to the take-outs on NH 16, to venture into Umbagog Lake, or to continue a few miles farther down the Androscoggin.

Umbagog Lake to Errol Landing (3¾ miles)

The short Androscoggin stretch flows leisurely through extensive marshes formed by ponding behind Errol Dam. Three miles from the channels to Umbagog you can find a launching ramp on the right where the river approaches NH 16 (mi. 19). Take out here, or paddle another ¾ mile to a second ramp (mi. 19¾) on the left bank ¼ mile above Errol Dam.

Umbagog Lake

Nearly 8 miles long and from 1 to 2 miles wide, the relatively shallow Umbagog straddles the Maine–New Hampshire boundary. Unlike most of New Hampshire's larger lakes, Umbagog has escaped the ravages of summer-home and recreational development. Its shoreline presents an almost unbroken vista of woodlands and wetlands set against a backdrop of fir-studded hills. Moose feed quietly nearby; bald eagles, ospreys, and loons nest along its banks; brook trout, salmon, and pickerel swim beneath its surface. However, the lake is heavily used by nature seekers, and campsites, which must be reserved in advance, may be hard to come by.

The sparkling blue waters of Umbagog hide another natural resource. On its bottom rests a thick layer of muddy diatomaceous earth, lending credence to the Indian translation of "Umbagog" as "muddy waters." Formed over thousands of years from skeletons of microscopic algae, diatomite is a valuable, silica-rich mineral used in a variety of industrial and domestic filtering processes and as an abrasive in cleansers and polishers.

To reach Umbagog Lake, paddle up one of the side channels that lead off from the Magalloway. This brings you to the swampy northwestern end of the lake. This side of Umbagog has two established campsites; the first is to the left on one of the small, marshy islands that divide the channels. The second, Moll's Rock, is on the western shore 1½ miles south of the outlets and is very popular.

Umbagog's eastern shore is rocky and offers many fine spots for swimming and picnicking. Several attractive campsites are along this shore.

The Rapid River enters Umbagog Lake at its northeastern end. You might want to paddle a couple of miles up this river to the lower end of the rapids. There are campsites on both banks, and a trail up the right bank leads to the dirt tote road that runs between Sunday Cove on Umbagog Lake and Richardson Lake and past the former home of author Louise Dickinson Rich.

The rapids above the campsites provide an excellent opportunity for novices to practice setting, ferrying, and other canoeing skills. They are popular for this purpose, and groups from nearby summer camps often spend whole days here. To run the rapids, unload at one of the campsites and then paddle, track, or carry your canoe upstream as far as you wish.

Bennett Covered Bridge, built in 1901, below Wilson's Mills

Instead of returning to the Magalloway to take out, you can paddle to the extreme southern end of Umbagog to the state-owned launching ramp just inside the New Hampshire border on NH 26 east of Errol.

2

Androscoggin River

Miles	Cumulative Miles	Breakpoints	River Rating	Special Difficulties
	0	Errol Dam		
½			2	
	½	Clear Stream		
3¾			F,Q	
	4¼	Mollidgewock Campground		
4¾			Q,1,2	
	9	Seven Islands Bridge		
9			F,Q	Dam*
	18	Pontook Dam		
3½			Q,2,3	
	21½	Dummer		
9¼			Q	
	30¾	Berlin		
* Does not require portage if taking out at breakpoint.				

The Androscoggin River between Errol and Berlin is one of the most popular—and crowded—canoeing rivers in New Hampshire. It is the only long run in the state with both clean waters and good-sized waves that can dependably be run throughout the summer. The section described here contains three distinct stretches of rapids. The first runs below Errol Dam for

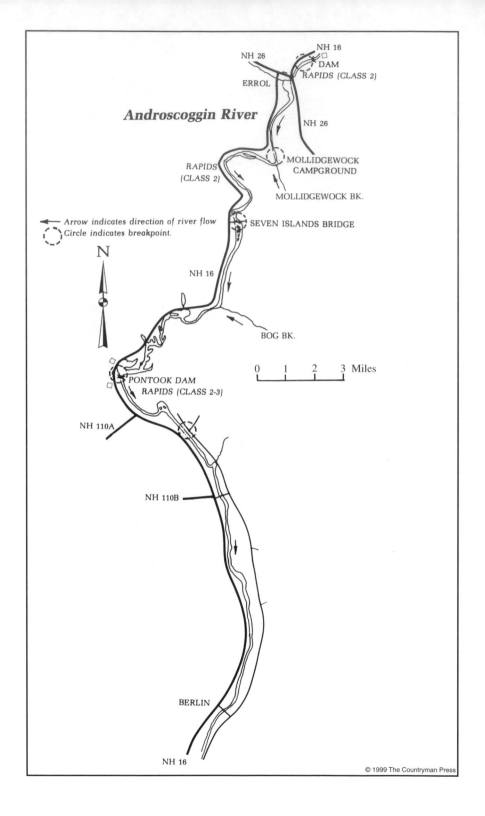

Androscoggin River

NH 26 NH 16
ERROL DAM
RAPIDS (CLASS 2)
NH 26

RAPIDS
(CLASS 2)

MOLLIDGEWOCK
CAMPGROUND

MOLLIDGEWOCK BK.

Arrow indicates direction of river flow
Circle indicates breakpoint.

SEVEN ISLANDS BRIDGE

N

NH 16

BOG BK.

0   1   2   3 Miles

PONTOOK DAM
RAPIDS (CLASS 2-3)

NH 110A

NH 110B

BERLIN

NH 16

© 1999 The Countryman Press

Class 2 rapids on the Androscoggin

½ mile, the second below Mollidgewock Campground for 3 miles, and the third below Pontook Dam for about 2 miles. Between these rapid sections are extensive stretches of quickwater and flatwater. Liveries along NH 16 below Errol rent canoes and provide instruction, and several campsites in the area are accessible to both car and canoe. Mollidgewock Campground is administered by the state of New Hampshire (603-788-3155).

The rapids of the Androscoggin are easier than the size of the river and height of the waves might lead you to expect, because they are usually run in the summer when the water is warm; this eliminates the very real danger of spills in chilled waters. Because there are few rocks, little skill in maneuvering is required; the rapids are short with good pools below for rescue, and many people are nearby to render assistance should anything go wrong. Also, because the road and your car are normally close by, you do not need to carry your dry pack.

The chief danger of canoeing on the Androscoggin is the false confidence it creates. Although you can safely wash down these rapids forward, backward, or even sideways, people who arrive at the bottom more or less intact think they have learned something about running rapids. When they run afoul of rocks in other rivers, they blame the "lack of water" and not their own lack of skill.

A quieter stretch on the Androscoggin River below Pontook Dam

Large lakes and dams keep the water flow on the Androscoggin relatively constant over the season. Minimum flow is only half the average, and the average flow on the Androscoggin would be considered high on most rivers. People used to the Androscoggin often think other rivers are too low because rocks are showing, when in fact they can be dangerously high.

The Androscoggin from Errol to Berlin is seldom run as a canoe camping trip. The standing waves in the rapids tend to fill a loaded canoe, and in any case the campsites along the right bank are readily accessible by car since NH 16 closely follows the river.

While it is possible, and to my mind preferable, to run straight through from Errol Dam to Pontook Dam (it saves a lot of loading and unloading), most people run exclusively either the big rapids or the easier in-between stretches.

Errol Dam to Clear Stream (Rapids) (½ mile)

Put in on the right just below Errol Dam at the pool by NH 16. The rapid below the pool is about ¼ mile long and is crossed about halfway down by the NH 26 bridge. If you are only running rapids, take out on the right in the field just above the mouth of Clear Stream (mi. ½). There can be a considerable traffic jam here on a good summer weekend.

Clear Stream to Mollidgewock Campground (3¾ miles)

If you are not running the rapids, put in at the take-out by Clear Stream mentioned above. Just under 4 miles of smooth water carry you to a take-out at Mollidgewock Campground (mi. 4¼), easily spotted on the right.

Mollidgewock Brook enters at the point from the left where the river turns right and the rapids start. Both it and Bog Brook (mi. 12) offer a mile or more of interesting paddling through a marsh, the distance limited only by your enthusiasm for dragging your canoe up over beaver dams and under bushes.

Mollidgewock Campground to Seven Islands Bridge (Rapids) (4¾ miles)

To run the second set of rapids, put in above Mollidgewock Campground, located on a loop of the old highway 3 miles south of Errol. Along the first 3 miles of this section, smooth water alternates with class 2 rapids that have standing waves. The rapids become easier over the last 1¾ miles. Since the road follows the river closely here, you can take out wherever you choose.

Seven Islands Bridge to Pontook Dam (9 miles)

You can select your own put-in along this stretch from NH 16. A class 2 rapid lies under the private Seven Islands Bridge (mi. 9). Quickwater follows, becoming slower as you progress downstream. Bog Brook enters on the left (mi. 12) opposite a turnout at the sharp turn in NH 16. The last 5 miles are largely backwater formed by Pontook Dam (mi. 18). Take out on the right from a pool adjacent to NH 16, well above the dam. There is a boat ramp and parking area at the dam, just off NH 16.

Pontook Dam to Dummer (Rapids) (3½ miles)

Pontook Dam has been rebuilt for power generation, and the water level in the rapids is not as reliable as in the upper river. Put in on the right below the dam. These rapids are the most difficult of the three, with larger rocks and waves. The rapids run for about 2 miles and are followed by quickwater. If you are not continuing to Berlin, you can take out on the right bank (mi. 20). Stay on the first road and don't trample the hay field. An alternate take-out is farther downstream on the left near the Dummer-Milan town line (mi. 21½).

Dummer to Berlin (9¼ miles)

If you avoided the rapids, put in from an access off a side road on the left bank near the Dummer-Milan town line (mi. 21½), about 2½ miles above the Milan bridge. This long, unobstructed run to Berlin is largely quickwater with occasional riffles. Take out on the right at the recreation area at 27½ miles, or at the playground on the left bank below the first bridge in Berlin (mi. 30¾).

Below Berlin

River cleanup efforts have greatly improved the quality of the river below Berlin. Therefore, it is now feasible to paddle on the lower parts of the Androscoggin into Maine.

   This trip is not continuous to the trip above due to the dams in Berlin. Put in at the bridge in Shelburne where the Appalachian Trail crosses the Androscoggin River. The river is a pleasant class 1, gradually becoming quickwater and then slowing down. Occasionally an easy rapid appears. There are mountain views across open meadows. It is 36 miles to Rumford Point, with no obstructions; the first dam is 3 miles farther at Rumford. There is a campsite on the river at Bethel, halfway down.

~ 3 ~

Baker River

Miles	Cumulative Miles	Breakpoints	River Rating	Special Difficulties
	0	Wentworth		
6			1	
	6	West Rumney		
4			Q,1	Class 2 rapid
	10	Rumney		
10½			Q	
	20½	Plymouth		

The Baker River rises in the White Mountains near the summit of Mount Moosilauke and flows south and then east to join the Pemigewasset River at Plymouth. It is a small, clear mountain stream going in to Wentworth, where it then slows down and begins to meander across the valley floor. While it is more popular during the spring months in high water, it can also be run in a normally wet summer. Its banks are largely wooded, with occasional houses along the way. The Baker is often used for float trips by students from Plymouth State College and is a good river to run in combination with the lower Pemigewasset.

Although the Baker was followed by Indians on their way to Montreal and was undoubtedly known also to white trappers, its existence was not recorded until 1712, when Lieutenant Thomas Baker led an expedition of 32 men up the Connecticut River to the small settlements near Haverhill and then returned down the river that now bears his name.

The Baker was an important link in the early colonial route from the

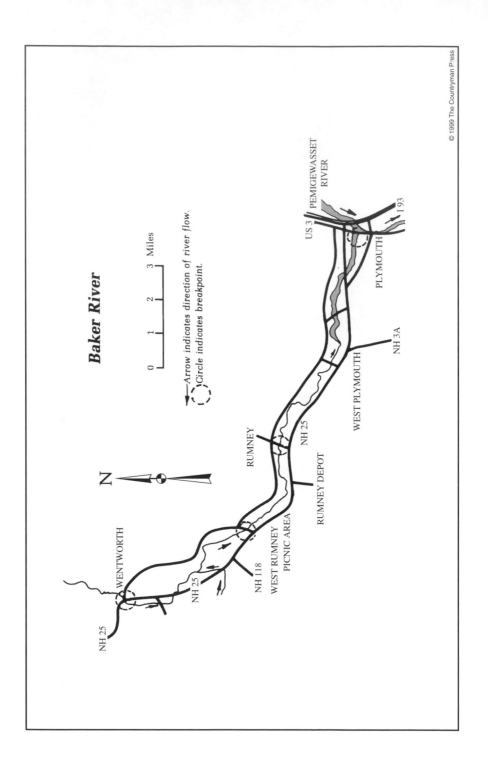

Baker River

Arrow indicates direction of river flow.
Circle indicates breakpoint.

0   1   2   3   Miles

N

NH 25

WENTWORTH

NH 25

NH 118

WEST RUMNEY
PICNIC AREA

RUMNEY DEPOT

RUMNEY

NH 25

WEST PLYMOUTH

NH 3A

US 3

PEMIGEWASSET
RIVER

PLYMOUTH

I 93

© 1999 The Countryman Press

Tubing is pleasant on a warm August day.

New Hampshire seacoast to the northern settlements along the Connecticut. The original trail led north past Lake Winnipesaukee through Sand-
wich Notch to Campton on the Pemigewasset and then up the Baker River
valley. In 1764 construction was authorized for the Coos Road, which ran
from Haverhill down the Baker valley to the coastal region. This first road to
New Hampshire's northern settlements was completed in 1767. Forty years
later, in 1804, a survey party exploring the alternate and higher route
through Franconia Notch discovered the Old Man of the Mountain.

Wentworth to West Rumney (6 miles)

The ballpark off NH 25 on the left bank below the bridge at Wentworth is a
convenient place to begin a trip down the Baker River, although in low
water this 6-mile stretch is too shallow and rocky to run. Fallen trees are
often a problem. The Baker passes beneath a small bridge across a narrow
gorge (mi. 1¼) and the NH 25 bridge (mi. 2) before reaching West Rumney
(mi. 6).

West Rumney to Rumney (4 miles)

In low water when the preceding stretch cannot be run, put in below the
steel bridge at West Rumney. Here the Baker becomes deeper and slower,

Time for a fancy French braid after breakfast

and while you may have to wade occasionally, the clear water and sandy, rocky bottom invite swimming in any case.

A highway picnic area with some facilities and good parking also offers access 1¼ miles farther downstream. Another ½ mile brings you to the (hardly noticeable) remains of a 3-foot dam that lie around a blind corner to the left (mi. 7¾). A short class 2 rapid is below it. The right bank with a visible gauging station is the best side on which to line or carry. A fast current continues for 2¼ miles to the bridge to Rumney (mi. 10).

A mile before the bridge, Rattlesnake Cliff, rising to the north directly above the river, is often used by rock climbers. A steep trail leads ⅕ mile to its summit from the west, offering a panorama of the river valley. The trailhead is on the road on the northern side of the river 2½ miles west of Rumney village at a historical marker.

Rumney to Plymouth (10½ miles)

You can avoid all the rapids by putting in at the Rumney bridge. The Baker continues to flow quickly past low cutbanks through rural countryside with excellent views of Stinson Mountain to the north. The (former) Smith covered bridge site (mi. 16) 6 miles below Rumney offers good access, but the high NH 25 bridge farther downstream (mi. 18½) does not. The current becomes slower over the last 3 miles. It is possible to take out at Plymouth on the right, upstream of the US 3 bridge (mi. 20¼), where a dirt track leads to the river. A railroad bridge crosses just below the US 3 bridge, and the current picks up again over the short distance to the Pemigewasset (mi. 20½). A better take-out is on the right below the bridge over the Pemigewasset River in Plymouth near I-93, exit 25 (see chapter 4).

4

Pemigewasset River

Miles	Cumulative Miles	Breakpoints	River Rating	Special Difficulties
	0	Plymouth		
16			F,Q	Dam*
	16	Ayers Island Dam		
1½			2,3	
	17½	Below Bristol Bridge		
10½			F,Q,1	Dam*
	28	Franklin Falls Dam		
2½			F,2	Dam
	30½	Winnipesaukee River		
* Does not require portage if taking out at breakpoint.				

The Pemigewasset River rises in Franconia Notch, flows south to the Winnipesaukee River in Franklin, and becomes the Merrimack. The upper river can be run only in very high water, but along most of its length below Plymouth, where the Baker joins the Pemigewasset, canoeing is possible almost anytime. The one exception is the 1½-mile stretch immediately below Ayers Island Dam, 16 miles south of Plymouth.

The origin of the name "Pemigewasset" is unclear. One theory is that it came from the Indian words *penaquil* (crooked), *wadchu* (mountain), *cooash* (pine), and *auke* (place), which different sources variously render as "crooked pine place in the mountains," "crooked mountain pine place," and

Pemigewasset River - part 1

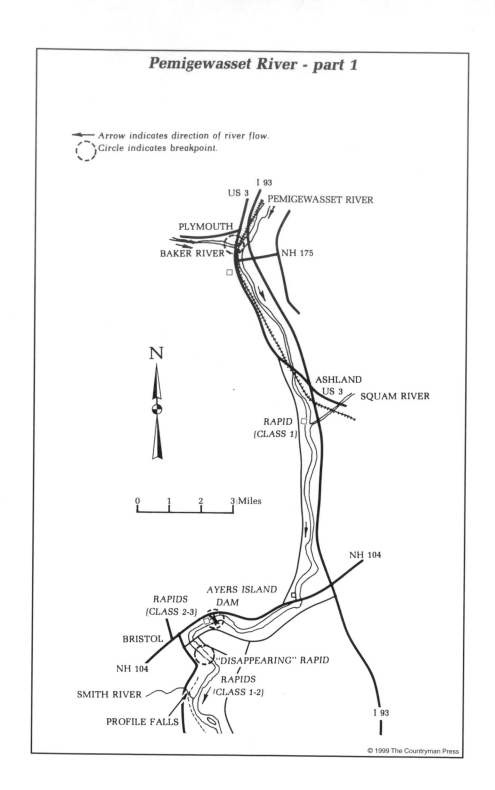

Arrow indicates direction of river flow.
Circle indicates breakpoint.

I 93

US 3

PEMIGEWASSET RIVER

PLYMOUTH

BAKER RIVER

NH 175

N

ASHLAND
US 3

SQUAM RIVER

RAPID
(CLASS 1)

0   1   2   3 Miles

NH 104

RAPIDS
(CLASS 2-3)

AYERS ISLAND
DAM

BRISTOL

NH 104

"DISAPPEARING" RAPID

SMITH RIVER

RAPIDS
(CLASS 1-2)

PROFILE FALLS

I 93

© 1999 The Countryman Press

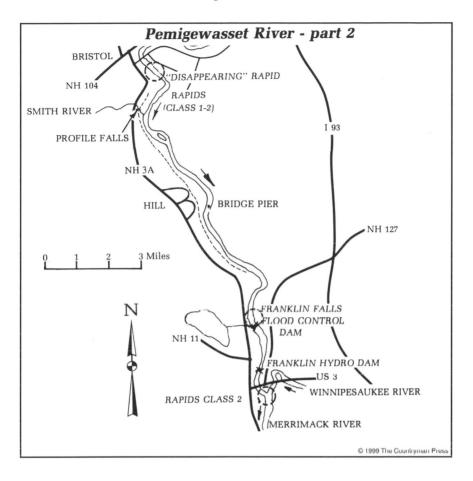

Pemigewasset River - part 2

so forth, depending on the arrangement of the words. A euphonious, if not especially accurate, translation is "valley of the winding water among the mountain pines." A simpler theory is that invading Abnaki named it in honor of their leader against the Iroquois.

Plymouth to Ayers Island Dam (16 miles)

Put in from the boat ramp in Plymouth ¼ mile downstream from the confluence with the Baker River and just below the bridge near I-93, exit 25. At the western end of the bridge, turn south into the municipal parking area. The boat access is at the northern end of the lot, where it is possible to drive down to the river.

The banks to Ayers Island are heavily wooded; no roads follow the river closely, so you see only a few houses.

When the Ayers Island Dam is full, its backwater extends nearly the full 16 miles to Plymouth. Under these conditions, the river slows down and deepens as it makes its way toward the dam. In summer the current usually continues about halfway, or a little more. The high US 3 bridge (mi. 5½) west of Ashland offers no access. Just below the mouth of the Squam River (mi. 7½), an easy class 2 rapid, Sawhegenet Falls, straddles a small island. This is a town of Bridgewater park, accessible down a dirt track from the road along the eastern bank. The gate may be locked. The current slows considerably below this point, and the strong afternoon wind is often from the west. A launching ramp (mi. 13½) on the right just above the NH 104 bridge offers access. Take out here or 2½ miles farther downstream on the right above the Ayers Island Dam (mi. 16). The dam lies just off NH 104.

One of my experiences with this stretch provides a classic example of why you should never unconditionally accept a river description given by anybody or any guidebook, including this one. Five different friends, each of whom had made the trip many times, swore on a stack of life jackets that the preceding description was correct, and it also agreed with Appalachian Mountain Club and Burmeister guidebooks. What better place, I thought, to take a couple of novices for a canoeing lesson!

If skiers can ski on wheels, why can't canoeists paddle on them?

The river did look a bit low when we parked our second car, but I had the description on unimpeachable authority and was more interested in making sure necessities were in the other car than in inspecting the river. The first half of the trip had more current than I had expected and extensive mud flats. When the "easy" class 2 rapid below the Squam River heralded its approach with a roar of white-water, I realized something was amiss—the dam had just been drawn down!

There was no convenient escape route, and my memory of the contours here was that the total drop was no more than 30 feet, of which we had already made 5 feet. This worked out to an average drop of only 5 feet per mile, so I chose to continue. However, inexperienced canoeists, anticipating the easier run when the dam is full, could have been in serious difficulty.

A river slowing down above a dam deposits sediment evenly over the bottom. Thus, when the channel widened, there was not enough water to float the canoe. The silt in suspension was like quicksand; we sank above our knees and had great difficulty pulling out. For the same reason, it was impossible to pole our way down. By fast footwork—easing out, shoving the canoe sideways, and jumping back in quickly—we managed to pass the shallow spots.

Beyond another set of rapids the river was cutting through even thicker layers of accumulated sediment. The suspended matter was reminiscent of the Colorado River, while the narrow channel caused standing waves. And every so often a yard or two of material sliding into the river from the unstable cliffs on the right produced more waves.

We were relieved to see the NH 104 bridge and our take out, but the fun was not yet over. The launching ramp by the bridge was still 30 unstable feet above our heads. A pie-in-the-face-style comedian could have made a good routine out of our efforts to drag the canoe—and ourselves—up the wet, slippery mudbank.

Ayers Island Dam to Below Bristol Bridge (1½ miles)

If you are running the 1½-mile stretch of rapids below Ayers Island Dam and are hand-carrying past the dam, follow a trail down the hill to the river. You can also reach this access by car; drive down a road behind the sheds and take a sharp left.

The rapids may not be runnable when the dam is closed, and when it is open they are a rocky class 2 to 3, 4 in heavy water; a successful run requires considerable skill. The left may be a better side to run along the upper part, and the most difficult drops are midway to the Bristol bridge (mi. 17).

I had been collecting information on this stretch for quite some time before running it myself. All my sources agreed that the 1-mile run from the dam to the Bristol bridge was class 2 to 3 in low water and even worse in high water. However, the ½-mile stretch below the bridge produced conflicting stories. Some said the rapids were easier, some said they ended altogether, while others claimed that a very difficult drop with high standing waves made the rapids impossible to run in an open canoe without swamping. Ratings ran from class 1 to class 4.

The "disappearing" rapid lies around a sweeping bend in the river below the bridge. Inexperienced canoeists and wave enthusiasts who follow the current around the outside of the curve encounter a long line of standing waves where the current hits a rocky ledge. The water here is deep with a good run-out into flattish water, so someone who doesn't mind taking in water may find this side of the rapid exciting to run.

On the other hand, experienced canoeists approaching prudently on the inside of the bend need only dodge a few rocks, and would scarcely notice the waves on the far side of the river. When low water makes the inside too rocky, you can run a line of smooth water adjacent to the waves.

Below Bristol Bridge to Franklin Falls Dam (10½ miles)

A side road on the left bank below the bridge at Bristol offers access below the big rapids around Bristol (mi. 17½). Short bits of fast water and occasional rocks appear over the next couple of miles to the mouth of the Smith River (mi. 19½), but beyond that the water gradually becomes slower and deeper. The possible ponding area of the Franklin Falls flood-control dam extends back to the Bristol bridge. No camping is permitted in the impoundment area, although day use is allowed.

The old town site of Hill, where piers are still clearly visible (mi. 23½), is on the right bank. The town was moved when the dam was built, as the area could be flooded.

The approach to Franklin Falls Dam (mi. 28) poses no problems. It can be seen ½ mile away and, like most flood-control dams, is drawn down (water has been released) at times when you would want to canoe. In addi-

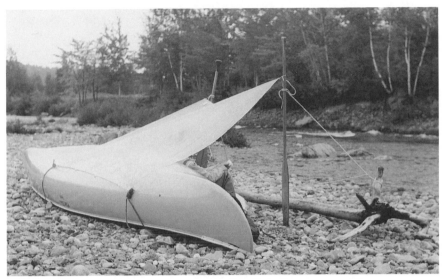

A tarp lean-to for a rainy, or sunny, day shelter. Note the canoe paddle.

tion, a log boom well above the dam shunts logs, debris, and canoeists onto the left bank. The dam area is clearly visible from NH 3A on the right, but the only access is from NH 127 on the left. Watch for a sign 2 miles north of Franklin. If you receive permission to drive through the gate and down to the water, the take-out here is easy, and unless you plan to continue down the Merrimack, this would be a likely spot to end your trip. Keep your vehicle on the hard road; the ground by the water is soft, and odds and ends of debris (such as boards with sharp nails) are scattered around.

Franklin Falls Dam to Winnipesaukee River (2½ miles)

To put in below the dam, continue down the dirt road noted above to the water. The total portage is ¾ mile. After 1½ miles, you reach the Franklin Hydroelectric Dam (mi. 29½), which should be portaged on the right. NH 3A gives access here below the dam. Class 2 rapids continue for 1 mile under the US 3 bridge in Franklin to the confluence with the Winnipesaukee and the start of the Merrimack River (mi. 30½)

5

Merrimack River

Miles	Cumulative Miles	Breakpoints	River Rating	Special Difficulties
	0	Winnipesaukee River		
17½			F,Q,1	
	17½	Sewall's Falls Road		
4¼			Q,2	see text
	21¼	Concord		
20½			F,Q	2 dams
	42¼	Manchester		Dam*
10			F,Q,2	2 ledges (class 3)
	52¼	Merrimack		
7¼			F,Q	
	59½	Nashua		

* Does not require portage if taking out at breakpoint.

The Merrimack River begins where the Pemigewasset and Winnipesaukee Rivers join in Franklin. Flowing south through central New Hampshire, it passes Concord, the state capital, and heavily industrialized Manchester and Nashua before entering Massachusetts. There it turns northeast, runs parallel to the New Hampshire border, and reaches the Atlantic Ocean at Newburyport. Like many big rivers draining northern New England, the Merrimack was once a major route to the interior for Indians, early colonists, and commercial steamboat companies. The river current is

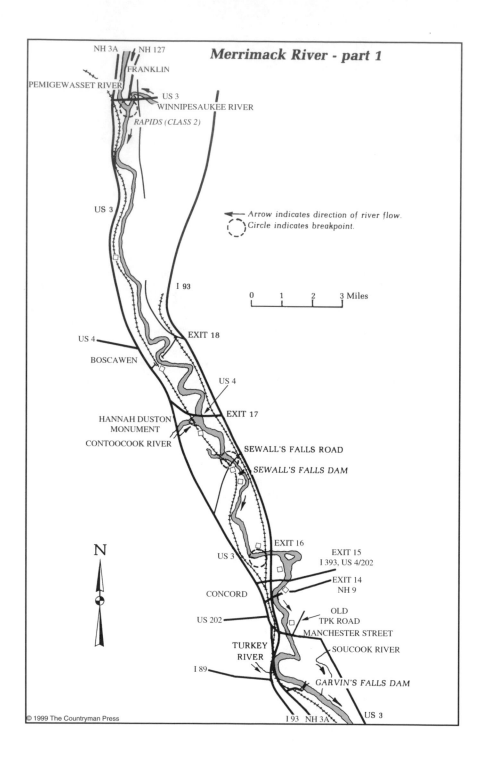

Merrimack River - part 1

NH 3A   NH 127

FRANKLIN

PEMIGEWASSET RIVER

US 3

WINNIPESAUKEE RIVER

RAPIDS (CLASS 2)

US 3

Arrow indicates direction of river flow.
Circle indicates breakpoint.

I 93

0   1   2   3 Miles

EXIT 18

US 4

BOSCAWEN

US 4

EXIT 17

HANNAH DUSTON
MONUMENT

CONTOOCOOK RIVER

SEWALL'S FALLS ROAD

SEWALL'S FALLS DAM

EXIT 16

US 3

EXIT 15
I 393, US 4/202

EXIT 14
NH 9

N

CONCORD

US 202

OLD
TPK ROAD

MANCHESTER STREET

SOUCOOK RIVER

TURKEY
RIVER

I 89

GARVIN'S FALLS DAM

US 3

I 93   NH 3A

generally slow, and the water is usually high enough to run throughout the summer. The towns along the Merrimack have followed the construction of sewage treatment plants with an upsurge of interest in the river, and many new parks and accesses have been built, with more in the planning stage. The upper stretches combine well with camping trips taken down the Baker and Pemigewasset Rivers (see chapters 3 and 4).

Winnipesaukee River to Sewall's Falls Road (17½ miles)

The put-in for a trip down the Merrimack is located on the eastern side of the Winnipesaukee River. Take River Road south from US 3 just on the eastern end of the Winnipesaukee River bridge. In 0.4 mile, just before the pumping station, turn on a dirt road down to the river. The banks are wooded along the ¼-mile run to the Pemigewasset and the start of the Merrimack.

The first 2 miles on the Merrimack have four short, class 1 rapids. The water is clear and pleasant, flowing through woodlands interrupted by an occasional cornfield or house. Much of the left bank belongs to the Gold Star Sod Farm, and you can sometimes hear traffic from nearby roads.

People wishing an easier start or a short trip can use the launching ramp 6 miles south of Franklin, which is below the rapids. It is reached by car from US 3. Take the dirt track 0.4 mile north of the Merrimack County buildings. The former bridge at Boscawen (mi. 11) is closed but offers access to the river at both ends; the better access is on the right. Take Depot Street from the southern end of Boscawen down to a park on the right downstream of the bridge, with a launching ramp at its southern end. To reach the left end of the bridge opposite the town, take exit 18 from I-93 west down a very steep hill to the river. Poison ivy is abundant.

The river bottom is clean and sandy, and the river meanders pleasantly past high cutbanks. Near Penacook the high bridge (mi. 15) connecting I-93 (exit 17) to US 3/4 crosses the Merrimack just above the old bridge, only half of which remains. The right half, which belonged to Boscawen, was sold for scrap.

Immediately below, the Contoocook River enters from the right. On the small island in the river's mouth stands a monument to Hannah Duston, who was captured by Indians from her home in Haverhill, Massachusetts, and carried up the river toward Canada. During the night of March 30, 1697, Hannah Duston, her midwife, and a 14-year-old boy scalped their sleeping

A rope swing is a popular fun break.

captors and escaped at the crack of dawn by canoe back down the Merrimack. While their trip upstream had taken 10 days, their journey to safety required only 2. Both trips must have been exceedingly difficult and chilly, because the river runs high in March and is still clogged by ice floes. A friend and I wondered which of the three had the skill to run the many rapids; the dams, of course, had not been built, but certainly the Hooksett and Amoskeag Falls could not have been run even then, and the other rapids would have required considerable canoeing knowledge to negotiate. My son pointed out that it took us more than 2 days (in early April) to travel the distance the three made in only one, but then they did have a strong incentive and a very early start!

Access to the river from the "park and ride" and parking for the island is poor. A good canoe-launching area is on the right bank below the island and above the sewage treatment plant. Reach this by crossing the bridge over the Contoocook River then taking the next left, a right at the end of the road, and the next left across the railroad tracks. Lowering the water level at the dam has caused an easy rapid to appear just above the Sewall's Falls bridge. Good access is available here on the right below the bridge on Sewall's Falls Road, where you can drive almost to the water (mi. 17½).

Sewall's Falls Road to Concord (4¼ miles)

The largest log crib dam in the country was breached in the spring of 1984 (mi. 18½). This caused the river to drop to its natural level in medium and low water and exposed the class 2 rapids from just above the Sewall's Falls bridge to the dam. At present the whole stretch, including the breach in the dam, can be run. A recreation area at the island has access to the river both above and below the dam site on the right.

A few riffles continue below the dam, and then the river is smooth to the first of the ramps in Concord, at exit 16 (mi. 21¾).

Concord to Manchester (20½ miles)

Concord has four launching ramps. The first, on the left bank upstream of the railroad bridge, is just above the I-93 bridge. This access can be reached from exit 16 of I-93. Exit west, cross the railroad tracks, and turn left at the T-intersection toward the river. The Society for the Protection of New Hampshire Forests (SPNHF) is high on the left side of the river below the bridge. At the large island it is 2 miles to the right and 3 miles around the left to the launching ramp just above the I-393 bridge. Along this stretch are numerous muskrats and birds. Below the I-393 bridge cutbanks tower above the river on the left. The Morton State Office and State Supreme Court buildings overlook the river here.

The third launching ramp (mi. 24) is on the left bank just above the Bridge Street bridge, at exit 14 of I-93, in the parking lot of the Everett Arena. The skyline of Concord with the capitol dome rises on the right.

The fourth launching ramp (mi. 25¼) lies in a deep cove on the left above a picnic area upstream of the Manchester Street bridge, which carries US 3 to exit 13 of I-93. Farther downstream, where NH 3A comes close to the river, the inundated Turkey Falls at the mouth of the Turkey River cause some turbulence.

Shortly beyond, a building on the right and an abutment on the left mark the Garvin's Falls Dam (mi. 28½). Land just above the dam on the left for an easy carry. This is a possible access, since a heavy-duty vehicle can drive down a dirt track nearly to the top of the dam. Ordinary cars can drive on the right to a fair spot to launch.

The current along the 17-mile run to Manchester depends on the height of the water. Both the Soucook River (mi. 29¼), just beyond Garvin's Falls, and the Suncook River (mi. 32¼), 3 miles downstream, enter on the left. Two launching ramps are on the left, one above and one below the Suncook River.

Except for the town of Suncook, high on a hill to the left, the banks along this stretch show little sign of civilization.

On the right shore overlooking Hooksett stands the Pinnacle, the "interesting mountain" noted by Thoreau in *A Week on the Concord and Merrimack*. The view from this knob more than justifies the easy climb. After portaging the dam (see below), go west from the bridge in Hooksett to NH 3A, then north to Pine Street (the first street on the left), and take the first left off this street (Ardon Street). The trail to the summit starts at the circle at the end of the street.

After the "mountain" comes into view, start watching for the Hooksett Dam (mi. 34¼), which lies above the Hooksett bridge and is not easy to see in advance. Take out at the launching ramp in the eddy on the left. A confident canoeist who is hand-carrying in low water can continue along the left shore and take out just below the old bridge abutment. Carry down the paved road past the power station and parking area to another launching ramp.

You should exercise care at the river bend below Hooksett Dam, where you find an assortment of piers from an old bridge, a new bridge, and a railroad bridge. On the way to Manchester the I-93 bridge (mi. 39) crosses, but the banks are surprisingly wild until the last mile above the city. The paddle past the suburbs of Manchester is interesting for its view of houses, retaining walls, and piers along the banks. Take out on the right by a good parking area just above the high Amoskeag Bridge (mi. 42½) to carry around Amoskeag Dam.

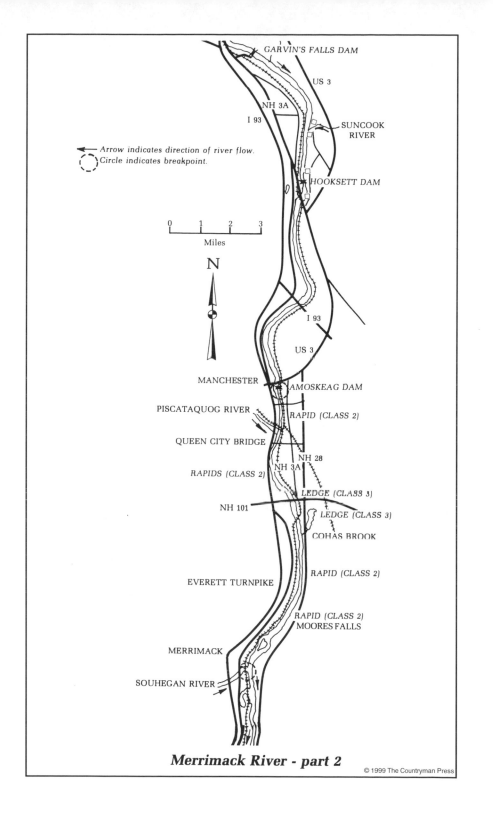

GARVIN'S FALLS DAM

US 3

NH 3A

I 93

SUNCOOK RIVER

HOOKSETT DAM

Arrow indicates direction of river flow.
Circle indicates breakpoint.

0   1   2   3
Miles

N

I 93

US 3

MANCHESTER   AMOSKEAG DAM

PISCATAQUOG RIVER   RAPID (CLASS 2)

QUEEN CITY BRIDGE

NH 28

NH 3A

RAPIDS (CLASS 2)

LEDGE (CLASS 3)

NH 101

LEDGE (CLASS 3)

COHAS BROOK

RAPID (CLASS 2)

EVERETT TURNPIKE

RAPID (CLASS 2)
MOORES FALLS

MERRIMACK

SOUHEGAN RIVER

Merrimack River - part 2

© 1999 The Countryman Press

Manchester to Merrimack (10 miles)

You can survey the rapids through Manchester both from the bridges and from the northbound lane of the Manchester bypass on the western bank (a link in the Everett Turnpike). Below the dam, factory walls rise sheer from the left side of the river, while the highway runs along a high bank on the right, but the noise of the water drowns out other sounds. The dam controls the water level here, and the run is easiest in fairly high water when a canoe can slide smoothly along the right bank. A practice slalom course is provided in this area. The rapids decrease as you pass through Manchester, ending with fast water. The two riverside parks on the left offer some access.

Back in the early 1800s a canal made it possible for boats to float all the way to Hooksett. This boat canal was not the mill canal—which was at the level of Canal Street and has now been mostly filled in—but down at river level. One remaining part that can be identified is on the left above the Granite Street bridge; from the shore you can see it upstream of Loeb Park. An alert canoeist can spot remnants of it at several of the rapids.

The Piscataquog River comes in from the right just above the Queen City Bridge (mi. 44).

Launching canoes at the county ramp in Boscawen

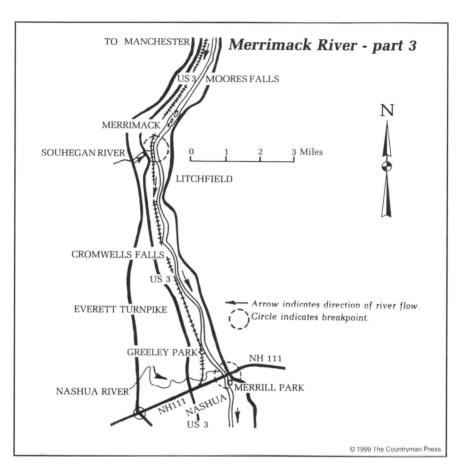

One and one-half miles below the Queen City Bridge you reach an easy riffle, and 1 mile below that, just beyond an island, the high NH 101 bridge (mi. 46½). The class 3 ledge below can be run on either side, but not down the middle. A new pipe across the river makes this drop more difficult than it was formerly. The ledge ¾ mile beyond, under the railroad bridge, is best run on the left at most water stages. You can inspect it from side roads on either side; access is possible on the right. Shortly past this last ledge, Cohas Brook on the left cascades down Goff's Falls into the Merrimack.

If you have run the rapids this far, you need not inspect the next two rapids. The first lies 1 mile below Cohas Brook beyond an island. The second, Moores Falls (mi. 50½), is much longer and lies below the second power line crossing. The right is usually a better side to run. Access is difficult along this stretch, since the few roads that come close to the river are on a high bank. Take out from the Souhegan River (mi. 54), which enters from the right, in the town of Merrimack.

Merrimack to Nashua (7¼ miles)

Most of this distance the river flows with a slow current. Only at Cromwells Falls does it speed up. On the right side is one of the few recognizable sections of the canal that used to bypass all the falls on the river.

In Nashua there is access at Greeley Park, where there is a boat ramp is on the right. Access is also possible below the NH 111 bridge on the left at Merrill Park.

6

Batten Kill

Miles	Cumulative Miles	Breakpoints	River Rating	Special Difficulties
	0	Hard Bridge		
5			F,Q	
	5	US 7A Bridge		
2			Q,2	
	7	Arlington		
26¾			Q,1	
	33¾	Center Falls, New York		Dam*

* Does not require portage if taking out at breakpoint.

The Batten Kill in southwestern Vermont is a beautiful, clear tributary of the Hudson River, and much of it can be run throughout a normally wet summer. Rising just north of Manchester, it flows southward along the Vermont Valley, sandwiched between the Green Mountains on the east and Mount Equinox on the west. From Arlington, where it turns abruptly west, it breaks through the Taconic Range to enter New York State, swinging south and then north in a wide S-shaped loop before joining the Hudson.

Spanned by four covered bridges, the sparkling waters of the Batten Kill tempt swimmers on a warm summer day, brook trout entice anglers to try their luck, and a fair but easy current speeds canoeists along their way. Below Manchester only one place could cause problems for the less skillful paddler. You can avoid this by starting instead at Arlington. From here, the river offers an easy 26-mile run in predominantly class 1 water. Two private

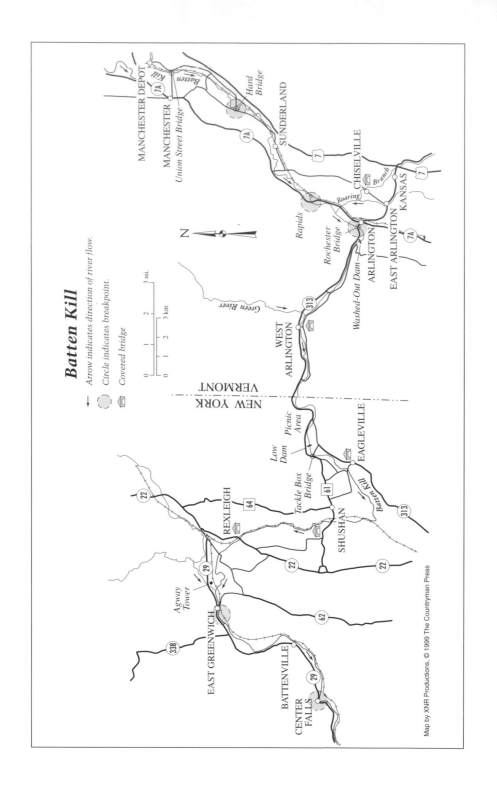

Batten Kill

Arrow indicates direction of river flow.

Circle indicates breakpoint.

Covered bridge

MANCHESTER DEPOT

MANCHESTER

Union Street Bridge

Batten Kill

Hard Bridge

SUNDERLAND

CHISELVILLE

Branch

Roaring

KANSAS

Rapids

Rochester Bridge

EAST ARLINGTON

ARLINGTON

Washed-Out Dam

N

Green River

WEST ARLINGTON

NEW YORK

VERMONT

Picnic Area

Low Dam

EAGLEVILLE

Tackle Box Bridge

Batten Kill

SHUSHAN

REXLEIGH

Agway Tower

EAST GREENWICH

BATTENVILLE

CENTER FALLS

3 mi.

3 km

Map by XNR Productions, © 1999 The Countryman Press

campgrounds front the river, one north of Arlington and the other on the southern loop near Shushan, New York.

The first 2¾ miles from Union Street in Manchester to the bridge on Richville Road are narrow, shallow, and badly obstructed with fallen trees. Therefore, it is better to start at the next bridge below Manchester.

Hard Bridge to US 7A Bridge (5 miles)

This stretch is less rocky than the previous section and holds fewer fallen trees and other obstructions. The surrounding countryside is mostly devoted to farming, with the land posted along much of the right bank and some of the left.

Below Sunderland (mi. 3) the current slows down somewhat, and the river deepens. The 2-mile run to the US 7A bridge (mi. 5) is pleasant, with some quickwater, some flatwater, and occasional riffles.

US 7A Bridge to Arlington (2 miles)

You can put in or take out at the US 7A bridge. A trail leads down to the river from a parking area on the left bank just below the bridge. Still relatively deep, the Batten Kill continues to flow slowly for a little over 1 mile. The current picks up just at the mouth of Roaring Branch (mi. 6), a side stream entering from the left. The river swings left, and a huge boulder sits toward the shore on the right. The rapid here is scratchy in low water, and in high water creates sizable waves (class 2). You may want to line or carry past this rapid on the right. A private campground is just below the rapid on the left.

Easy rapids continue for another ½ mile. At Arlington VT 313 crosses (mi. 6¼); the town golf course and a fishing access are on the right.

Arlington to Center Falls, New York (26¾ miles)

The old dam half a mile downstream from Arlington is almost gone and presents no problem, except for a few riffles. Here the Batten Kill turns sharply west to leave the Vermont Valley and flows through the breach in the Taconic Range. For the next 26 miles the river gradient drops almost evenly and a fast current riffles over small rocks, giving a smooth, pleasing ride. This lower portion can be run in all but the driest summers, which

A canoe table helps to keep sand out of the food. Block it up solidly to avoid spills.

may explain its popularity for float trips. Canoes find themselves sharing waters with all manner of craft, from fancy rubber rafts to inner tubes and air mattresses, and even an occasional log! With very little effort, you can cover the first 5 miles to the Arlington Green Bridge in about three hours. Less than 1 mile above the covered bridge, the milky green waters of the aptly named Green River (mi. 11¼) join the Batten Kill.

The Arlington Green Bridge, built in the 1850s, is the first of four covered bridges that cross the lower portion of the Batten Kill. Bridges appear regularly every couple of miles from here to Shushan.

Just across the New York State line a picnic area on the right offers a fair access. Below it log cribs extend out from the right bank, and a hill rises almost vertically on the left. The cribs were built recently to stabilize the shore and to improve fishing conditions. Both banks are posted against any use other than fishing access. The NY 313 bridge crosses at mile 14¾. The low dam just above the County 61 bridge (mi. 16¼) called the Tackle Box Bridge in reference to a former bait shop, can be run.

The river loops south in a giant arc around huge rocky cliffs before flowing north to Shushan. The mountains here consist of complex layers of different types of rock that have been subjected to repeated uplifting and folding. Erosional forces of glaciers and ancient streams have carved away the exposed weaker rock, leaving gaps and breaches in the mountain ridge. Today's Batten Kill, following the path of least resistance, flows around the harder structures left behind.

The old covered bridge at Eagleville (mi. 17¼) still carries traffic, but the one at Shushan (mi. 21¼) is now a local historical museum. It remains in place, but its original purpose is now served by a newer bridge located immediately upstream. A private campground is on the left about halfway between these two bridges, just before the County 64 bridge.

North of Shushan a railroad crosses and recrosses the Batten Kill. Near the height of its northern loop, an old mill (mi. 25½) still stands, although the dam that powered it has completely washed away. Immediately beyond, you pass beneath the fourth covered bridge. On warm days, watch for children leaping into the river from a hole in the bridge's siding. When the bridge was rebuilt in 1984, an "inspection door" was left in the wall.

Another ¾ mile brings you to the NY 22 bridge (mi. 26¾). You then pass yet another railroad bridge, and a tall cement Agway tower is visible on the right as you approach East Greenwich. Black Creek (mi. 27) enters

"Inspection door" in covered bridge

the Batten Kill here on the right. The dam at East Greenwich is gone now leaving a short rapid above the bridge. The best access is a quarter mile below the bridge on the right.

The river continues much the same—a fair current, occasionally spreading out, flowing through woods and cornfields—for another 5¾ miles. A few easy rapids start ¼ mile above Center Falls, New York. Take out on the right at an old abutment above the dam (mi. 33¾), parking is poor.

Otter Creek

Miles	Cumulative Miles	Breakpoints	River Rating	Special Difficulties
	0	South Wallingford		
3¾			Q,1,2	
	3¾	Wallingford		
15½			1,Q	
	19¼	Rutland		
1¼			F,Q,2	2 dams
	20½	Center Rutland		
7			F	Dam*
	27½	Proctor		
38			Q	Dam*
	65½	Middlebury		
12¼			F,Q,2	4 dams
	77¾	Lemon Fair		
* Does not require portage if taking out at breakpoint.				

Vermont's longest river, Otter Creek, rises west of the Green Mountain range only a few miles north of the source of the Batten Kill, one of the few New England rivers that flows northward for its entire length. It empties into Lake Champlain north of Vergennes.

Almost all of Otter Creek's canoeable stretches are quickwater with no

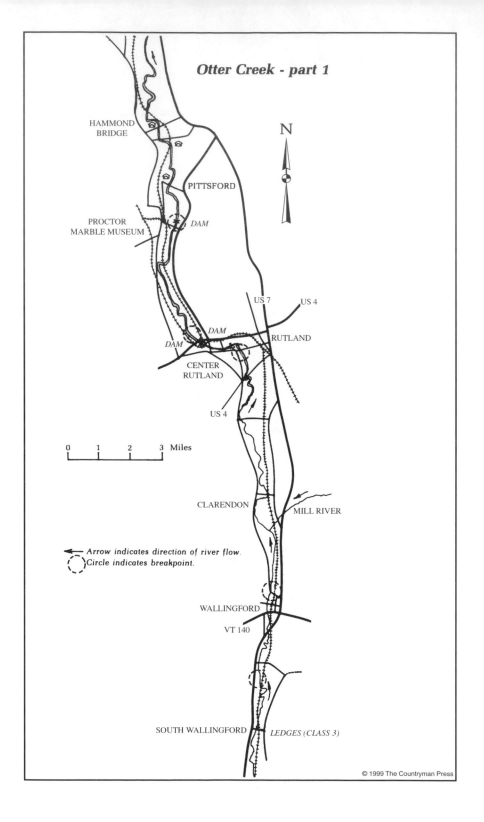

Otter Creek - part 1

HAMMOND
BRIDGE

N

PITTSFORD

PROCTOR
MARBLE MUSEUM

DAM

US 7   US 4

DAM

DAM   RUTLAND

CENTER
RUTLAND

US 4

0   1   2   3 Miles

CLARENDON
MILL RIVER

Arrow indicates direction of river flow.
Circle indicates breakpoint.

WALLINGFORD

VT 140

SOUTH WALLINGFORD   LEDGES (CLASS 3)

© 1999 The Countryman Press

rapids, since the river's drop is largely concentrated in unrunnable water-falls, the sites of which are now occupied by dams. Mountain views from the river are lovely, and even driving the car shuttle is delightfully scenic.

Although you can run Otter Creek from Danby or above after a rain when the water is high and muddy farther downstream, for most of the season it is better to begin at Wallingford or Center Rutland. These runs offer pleasant, easy paddling.

South Wallingford to Wallingford (3¾ miles)

The bridge at South Wallingford is a poor place to start, because the ledges extend under the bridge, and rapids continue. Instead start 1½ miles north, where US 7 approaches the river, just before a highway cut. The US 7 bridge (mi. 2) is high and on a long causeway.

Three bridges span the river in Wallingford. Below the VT 140 bridge, which is first, is a rocky rapid from rocks washed in by an industrious side stream on the right. An old canal on the right is best seen from the Mill Street bridge. The left-hand span of the last, River Road, bridge, at a right curve, is blocked by a ledge and perhaps also by debris extending into the right-hand side. And the current is fast. Riffles continue for some distance downstream.

Wallingford to Rutland (15½ miles)

If you want an easier trip you can put in below the third bridge in Wallingford. From here Otter Creek flows through valley farmland between steep, muddy banks. In 3½ miles, Mill River, which cuts through the main ridge of the Green Mountains at Clarendon Gorge, enters on the right. A small, shallow, sandy-bottomed pool has formed where the two rivers meet and makes a delightful spot for splashing around and getting wet on a warm day. Unless you are a very determined through-tripper, take out at River Street, the first Rutland bridge (mi. 19¼), the next bridge below the high US 4 bridge, and portage by car past the next two dams.

Rutland to Center Rutland (1¼ miles)

A quarter mile below the first Rutland bridge, the river passes over a low dam, visible from the road on the western bank. Although low, it is high enough to be dangerous but hard to see from the river, and people have washed over it by mistake. A rapid continues for ½ mile below with a bridge crossing overhead. The high dam at Center Rutland lies ½ mile below the rapid. Take out at the high double bridge, but expect a difficult climb up high, steep banks covered with small trees. The ½-mile carry can be made on either side; neither is particularly good, but the left is probably better. Carry down the railroad tracks through the factory yard, and then back to the river to the short rapid just below the dam (mi. 20½). Those carrying by car can put in on either bank from side roads.

Center Rutland to Proctor (7 miles)

After a little fast water below the high dam and rapid, the river runs flat for 7 miles to Proctor (mi. 27½), flowing past wooded banks and farmland. At Proctor, take out on the right at the bridge to portage around the dam. Carry down VT 3 on the right bank, turn left onto Patch Street partway down the hill, then turn left to the sewage treatment plant and left again onto the clay road before the gate. This road, which leads to the river, is drivable in dry weather. In wet weather the cascade below the dam is lovely, but in dry weather all the water is diverted into the factory.

The large building on the left bank is the Marble Museum, whose exhibits are open to the public (fee charged).

Proctor to Middlebury (38 miles)

Otter Creek from Proctor to Middlebury is a popular canoe run through rural Vermont countryside with occasional fine views of the Green Mountains to the right. The current is slow and free of difficulties, while frequent bridges offer easy access. The water tends to be somewhat muddy, so this is a better trip for nature lovers than swimmers. Yes, there are otters—we saw five—and bird lovers will be pleased. Explore an occasional side stream, which might lead to a little pond or a waterfall. This stretch of the river should appeal to covered bridge lovers; six of these wooden structures still cross the river, although some no longer carry traffic.

This long, unobstructed run ends at a dam in the college town of Middlebury (mi. 65½). Five dams between this take-out and the mouth of the Lemon Fair River require carries. Those who carry from here by car will

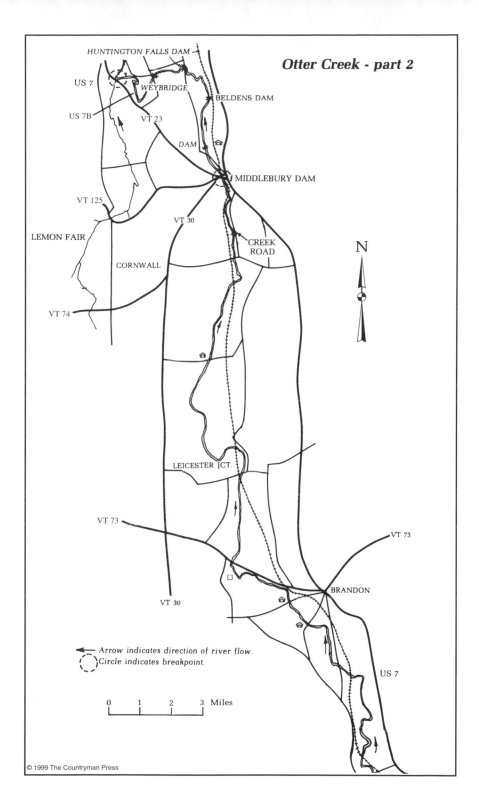

Otter Creek - part 2

HUNTINGTON FALLS DAM

US 7

WEYBRIDGE

US 7B

VT 23

BELDENS DAM

DAM

MIDDLEBURY DAM

VT 125

VT 30

LEMON FAIR

CREEK
ROAD

CORNWALL

N

VT 74

LEICESTER JCT.

VT 73

VT 73

VT 30

BRANDON

Arrow indicates direction of river flow.
Circle indicates breakpoint.

US 7

0   1   2   3 Miles

© 1999 The Countryman Press

find a safe and convenient water-level take-out 1½ miles above the town on the right. To reach the side road to this landing, drive south on US 7 from Middlebury and turn right onto Creek Road.

Middlebury to Lemon Fair River (12¼ miles)

Through-trippers who hand-carry past the dam at Middlebury should take out on the left as soon as they see the Middlebury bridge (or even before), because the dam is immediately below it. Carry up the bank, across the highway, and through a parking lot back down to the river. If you are carrying from here by car, you can load in the reserved parking lot on the left bank. Inspect the take-out by the dam in advance, since the current picks up above the bridge.

This stretch of Otter Creek contains four more dams in addition to the one at Middlebury and generally appeals only to portaging enthusiasts. All but the second dam, at Beldens, are below bridges and should be portaged on the left.

To run lower Otter Creek, you can put in at Weybridge (mi. 73½) either from the center of the island below the dam (which is not particularly easy) or from the right bank farther downstream. The river is predominantly quickwater from the dam to the mouth of the Lemon Fair (mi. 77¾). (See chapter 8.)

Helping the farmer drive his cows to pasture after milking.

~ 8 ~

Lemon Fair River–Otter Creek

Miles	Cumulative Miles	Breakpoints	River Rating	Special Difficulties
		Lemon Fair River		
	0	West Cornwall		
11¾			Q	
	11¾	Otter Creek		
		Otter Creek		
		Lemon Fair		
9			Γ,Q	Dam*
	20¾	Vergennes		
9			F,Q	
	29¾	Lake Champlain		
* Does not require portage if taking out at breakpoint.				

A trip down the Lemon Fair combines well with one on lower Otter Creek. Rising west of Brandon, the Lemon Fair flows parallel to and just west of Otter Creek and joins it about 4 miles below the Weybridge Dam. The water is generally uninviting for swimmers, but the river is a real delight to the nature lover. Don't let the muddy water discourage you; it is caused by the clay bottom and, oddly enough, is muddier in low water than in high. (On most rivers, waters are clearer in low water than in high, because the slower currents cause the sandier sediment to settle out.) Although people may consider the water undesirable, birds, animals, and fish thrive on it. A steady

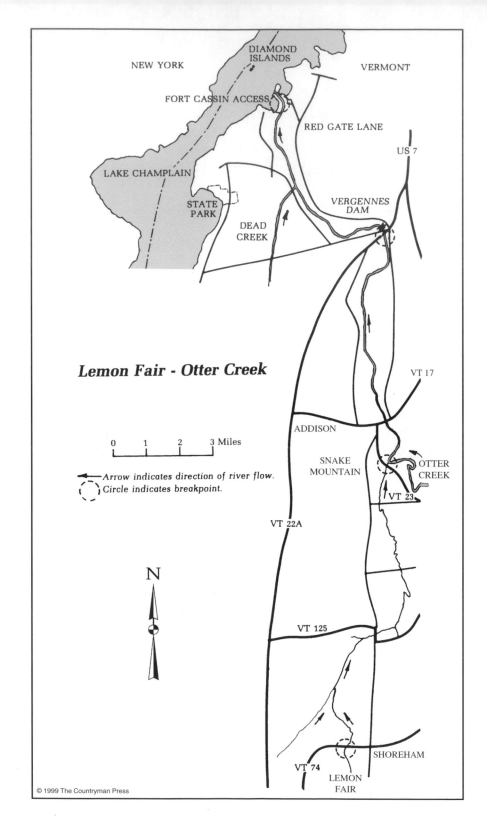

Lemon Fair - Otter Creek

NEW YORK

DIAMOND ISLANDS

VERMONT

FORT CASSIN ACCESS

RED GATE LANE

US 7

LAKE CHAMPLAIN

VERGENNES DAM

STATE PARK

DEAD CREEK

VT 17

ADDISON

SNAKE MOUNTAIN

OTTER CREEK

VT 23

VT 22A

0   1   2   3 Miles

Arrow indicates direction of river flow.
Circle indicates breakpoint.

N

VT 125

VT 74

SHOREHAM

LEMON FAIR

plop-plopping of startled muskrats, otters, turtles, and fish can be heard as the canoe approaches, and huge clouds of birds rise in advance. In fact, the whole river seems more like the Everglades than like Vermont. Many trees lining the banks have multiple trunks and intricate exposed root systems, and their branches sweep down over the river in a manner reminiscent of Florida's cypress and mangrove. If a submerged log were suddenly to open wide its jaws, it wouldn't seem a bit surprising.

Lemon Fair

West Cornwall to Otter Creek (11¾ miles)

Put in from the VT 74 bridge west of West Cornwall or, in low water, from the VT 125 bridge (mi. 4¾) farther downstream. The Lemon Fair winds across low-lying fields drained by canals and is somewhat obstructed by water plants and fallen trees, particularly above VT 125. Flocks of herons congregate to feed in an especially marshy stretch between two side-road

Canoe packed neatly for a trip on the Lemon Fair

bridges that cross the lower portion. You reach higher ground shortly before the VT 23 bridge and the confluence of the Lemon Fair with Otter
Creek (mi. 11¾).

Otter Creek

Lemon Fair River to Vergennes (9 miles)

A marble monument stands high on the left bank of Otter Creek ⅒ mile
upstream from the mouth of the Lemon Fair. Eight feet tall and surrounded
by an iron fence, it is set in a horse pasture between road and river and is
visible from both. The monument commemorates a raid in which Indians
and Tories attacked a small settlement, burned the buildings, and carried
the men and older boys off to Quebec. The women and children left behind
hid in a cellar for 10 days until they were rescued.

Otter Creek flows slowly and smoothly past farms and cornfields to Vergennes (mi. 20¾). A trailer park and houses appear on the right bank ½ mile
above the bridge; the dam at Vergennes lies just below the bridge and should
be scouted in advance, if possible. The best landing, on the right just above
the bridge, is close to the dam, and the current increases just as you reach it.
Do not attempt this take-out if you are inexperienced or the river is high.
The bank above this landing is overgrown and offers poor scouting or
portaging. From your chosen landing above the bridge, carry along the road
to the right up a steep hill. Watch for trucks barreling down the incline. Turn
left onto MacDonough Drive and carry for ⅒ mile to a public landing.

On this site during the War of 1812, the MacDonough shipyard con-
structed gunboats for use on Lake Champlain and also built the ship
Saratoga in only 40 days. This small fleet spent the winter of 1813 at But-
tonwoods, just above the mouth of Dead Creek. Because they feared that
the British would attempt to block Otter Creek's mouth, the Americans
made a dugway to Lake Champlain from the left bank of Dead Creek, but
it was never used.

Vergennes to Lake Champlain (9 miles)

Below the dam at Vergennes the river is deep and slow moving, and you
begin to see a few motorboats. In 4¾ miles Dead Creek enters on the left.

A blue heron is a common sight on many of these rivers.

You can paddle up this marshy stream in a state-operated wildlife refuge; this makes a fine side trip for avid bird-watchers. In high water the low bridge over the mouth of Dead Creek may not clear a canoe.

A short distance beyond Dead Creek are a few cottages, and the shores are posted against trespassing and fishing. Farther downstream the banks become swampy and continue so to Lake Champlain (mi. 29¾).

The last access on the river, the Fort Cassin fishing access, is located on the right off Red Gate Road ½ mile from the mouth of Otter Creek. Nothing remains of Fort Cassin, a former gun emplacement, but its foundations, and a private cottage now occupies the site. The river's current here is negligible.

Lake Champlain presently has no public campsites in the immediate vicinity of Otter Creek. Button Bay State Park is 6 miles to the south. For swimming, a sandy town beach is tucked deep in a cove between Otter and Little Otter Creeks.

Lake Champlain

This part of Lake Champlain is spectacular. If the weather permits, paddle north along the shore. The ledgy rock formations rise vertically from the water's edge and in places even overhang the lake, so that you can paddle directly under a cliff.

The lake at this point is nearly 2 miles wide, and if the weather is good you can venture across to the New York State shore. Remember, though, that large boats ply this lake and kick up a considerable wake. The Diamond Islands, minuscule rocky outcroppings, lie halfway across and just north of the mouth of Otter Creek. A white lighthouse marks the southernmost island.

The rock formations along the New York shore are quite different from those on the Vermont side. Split Rock Mountain rises steeply for hundreds of feet, and the area is uninhabited for miles in either direction. The steep, rocky shore makes it difficult to land and pull out a canoe in a heavy wind, and precious few places are even flat enough to sit on! This would be a poor place to get caught in a storm.

The views across the lake, however, are breathtaking. The Green Mountains, with Mount Mansfield and Camel's Hump, rise in the distance to the east and the high peaks of the Adirondacks to the west. Take along a good map to help identify them.

9

Winooski River

Miles	Cumulative Miles	Breakpoints	River Rating	Special Difficulties
	0	Montpelier		
5½			Q,1	Rapids, dam*
	5½	Middlesex		
16¾			F,Q,1,2	Dam
	22¼	Jonesville		
17			F,Q,1	Dam*
	39¼	Essex Junction		
4¼			F,Q,1	
	43½	Essex		
4			X	Recommend portage 2 dams and gorge
	47½	Winooski		
10			F,Q	
	57½	Lake Champlain		

* Does not require portage if taking out at breakpoint.

The Winooski is the most spectacular of the three big rivers that cut through the Green Mountain range. It rises in Vermont's eastern hills to flow westward past the state capitol in Montpelier and empties into Lake Champlain just north of Burlington. Except where it slices through its renowned, deep-walled gorges, the river flows smoothly across the valley farmlands and

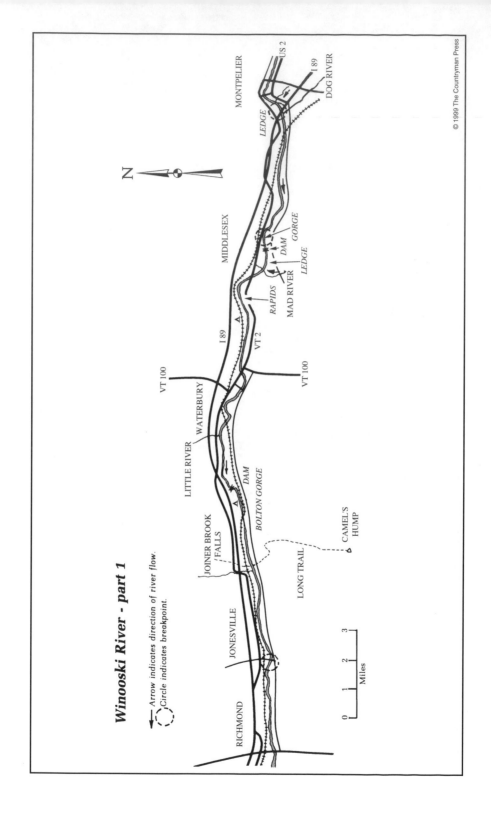

Winooski River - part 1

Arrow indicates direction of river flow.
Circle indicates breakpoint.

MONTPELIER

US 2

I 89

DOG RIVER

LEDGE

MIDDLESEX

GORGE

DAM

LEDGE

MAD RIVER

RAPIDS

N

I 89

VT 2

VT 100

VT 100

WATERBURY

LITTLE RIVER

DAM

BOLTON GORGE

JOINER BROOK / FALLS

CAMEL'S HUMP

LONG TRAIL

JONESVILLE

RICHMOND

0   1   2   3
Miles

the more expansive and fertile plains above Lake Champlain. The water is not as clean as one might hope, but the scenery makes it worthwhile.

Although the upper Winooski has some pleasant, short runs, several dams near Montpelier make that portion unsuitable for a lengthy canoe camping trip. Dams are less frequent below Montpelier, where the Winooski can be run throughout the summer, although in very dry years there may be some shallow spots. A car is highly desirable for the Essex and Winooski portages; it does not help at Bolton.

The Winooski Valley Park District (Ethan Allen Homestead, Burlington, VT 05401; 802-863-5744) has been working on a canoe trail on the Winooski and has signed some portages. The campsites offer no amenities, sometimes not even a sign. The upper ones are difficult if not impossible to find. The park district publishes a canoe and natural history guide that provides much interesting information.

Montpelier to Middlesex (5½ miles)

Below Montpelier put in from the right bank and from US 2 underneath the high I-89 bridge. The Dog River enters on the left. The run to Middlesex Gorge is pleasant with occasional riffles and one ledge probably best run on the right.

Below the Middlesex bridge (mi. 5½), keep to the left channel around the island and land on the left above the dam for a short carry.

Middlesex to Jonesville (16¾ miles)

The river valley begins to narrow at Middlesex, and beyond the dam the Winooski passes through a small gorge with sizable waves, which you can see in the distance from the put-in below the dam. The gorge offers no special difficulties other than high waves, and slack water below provides an opportunity to empty your canoe of excess water.

The Mad River empties into the Winooski about ½ mile farther downstream (mi. 6¼). There is a good swimming hole at the foot of the ledges ¼ mile upstream on the Mad River.

A class 2 ledge (more difficult in high water) lies around the corner downstream of the US 2 bridge (mi. 6¾). You can inspect this from a trail opposite a pull-off beyond the end of the high fence that starts below the

Bailing water out of the canoe with a bailer made from a plastic jug

US 2 bridge. High cliffs rise on one or both sides of the river with diminishing rapids for some distance downstream. At the far end a couple of old rings from logging days can be found in rocks in the center and on the left shore. From Waterbury to Bolton Falls the river flows peacefully across the narrow valley. You pass beneath another US 2 bridge (mi. 10¼), the first of three bridges in Waterbury, and 3 miles below town you come to the mouth of Little River (mi. 13¼), which drains Waterbury Reservoir to the right.

The portage at Bolton Falls is difficult, and most people portaging by car will wish to take out at the Winooski Street bridge in Waterbury or a preselected point from the dirt road on the southern bank. You must complete the portage at Bolton in order to take out there.

After another 2 miles or so, the river swings north and starts to drop through the magnificent Bolton Gorge (mi. 15½). Here the Winooski breaks through the Green Mountains' main ridge (Camel's Hump stands out boldly on the left) and cuts deeply through high rock cliffs to plunge over Bolton Falls. Strong current makes the approach very dangerous.

Take out on the left bank at the southern swing where the river starts to bend toward the gorge. You can just barely see the gorge here to the right, rapids lie ahead, and a power line runs across a hilltop. Barrels may mark the take-out. The portage trail leads circuitously around up the hill and down back to the river. The dam has been rebuilt, and a good road leads down to a picnic area and boat launching. The total portage is ¾ mile.

A short hike up the side road from the pool to the top of the cliff under the power line allows a tremendous view of the gorge and of Camel's Hump in the distance. The gorge is also visible from the eastbound lane of I-89 just before the rest area (but not from the westbound lane or from US 2).

The launch below the dam is easy. A campsite is on the right half a mile downstream.

Less than a mile beyond Bolton Gorge you reach a railroad bridge supported by four pilings (mi. 16¼). The five channels around them are sprinkled with rocks that cause trouble in low water, while the pilings themselves present problems in high water. (You can see this place from the road on the south.) From here to Jonesville the river is predominantly slow current.

The Long Trail originally came down Bamforth Ridge (mi. 18¾). At that time it met the Winooski 2½ miles below the railroad bridge, where there was no bridge. It was moved west to go over Robbins Mountain and cross the bridge at Jonesville, then east again down Honey Hollow. Now it has been returned to Bamforth Ridge. A new footbridge will be built across the Winooski River, along with a new trail on the north even farther east than the original.

Jonesville to Essex Junction (17 miles)

The Jonesville bridge (mi. 22¼), with an elevation of only 326 feet, is the Long Trail's lowest point.

The river flows smoothly with gradually diminishing current for the next 17 miles to Essex Junction. Camel's Hump can be seen to the southeast, and Mount Mansfield stands out boldly to the northeast. The Winooski valley opens up beyond the Richmond bridge (mi. 25½), and the river meanders back and forth across the broad plain. The I-89 and US 2 bridges cross together about 3 miles below Richmond (mi. 28½). Another 5¼ miles brings you to the North Williston bridge (mi. 33¾). The power dam at Essex Junction (mi. 39¼) lies 5½ miles farther downstream.

The best portage is on the right, and a car can be used. Take out on the right on the private road to IBM, at the CANOE PORTAGE sign. Cross VT 2A and turn left, then right on Cascade Road. Past Cascade Park, turn in left toward the plant, and park outside the fence. The portage circles to the right outside the fence to the river. It is no longer possible to drive all the way down. Should you wish to hand-carry, it may be very difficult to cross VT 2A safely.

Overlook Park, on the southern end of the bridge, has been furnished by the Green Mountain Power Company with tables, grills, and outhouses. (This is not the "campsite," which is on the river well upstream of the dam on the left, on the property of Morris Brown.) From the picnic area a rough trail slabs the steep rocks to the river.

Essex Junction to Essex (4¼ miles)

Class 1 water extends about ½ mile below the power dam. Muddy Brook park is on the left a mile below the dam, and offers a waterfall and nature trails as well as an easy take-out. The river twists for another 3 miles of faster water before the current begins to pick up leading into Winooski Gorge. The old boat ramp at the top of the northern loop has been closed. You must carry ¼ mile up from there at Woodside Park to a parking area.

Woodside Park is ½ mile east of the Fanny Allen Hospital on VT 15, the southern extension at a crossroads with a small sign: TOWN OF ESSEX RECRE-ATION LAND. Follow it down to the parking area.

Essex to Winooski (4 miles)

It might be possible to paddle to the sewage treatment plant another mile downstream on the right and take out there. Check in advance. There is no access at Lime Kiln Road, which provides a scenic view of the sheer cliffs it crosses. A dam lies in the next gorge ½ mile downstream of this bridge, which is not feasible to carry past at that point. Rapids continue under the interstate bridge, with cascades above the dam in Winooski. An additional hazard is that what you see is not necessarily what you get: The water level is controlled by the dam at Essex Junction, so it can rise suddenly, greatly increasing the force of the current.

Winooski to Lake Champlain (10 miles)

From the previous take-out, continue west on VT 15 to the road that crosses the bridge in Winooski. Turn left, then right onto West Canal Street, on the

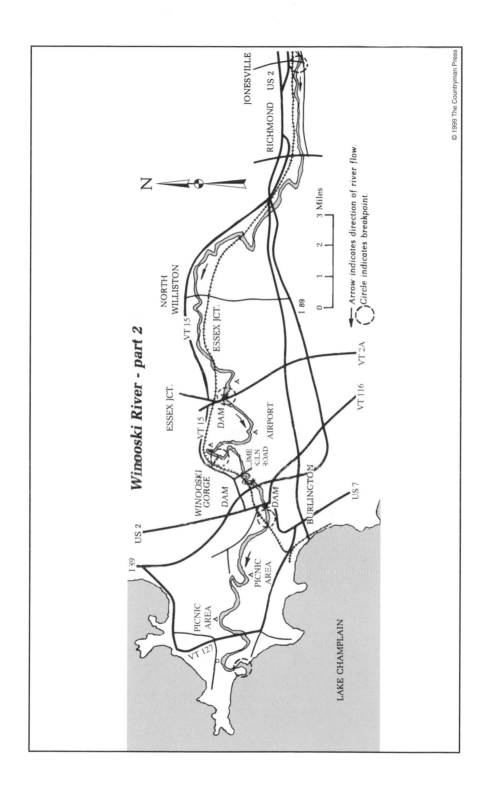

Winooski River - part 2

N

PICNIC AREA

I 89

US 2

WINOOSKI GORGE
DAM

VT 127

PICNIC AREA

PICNIC AREA

ESSEX JCT.

NORTH WILLISTON

VT 15

ESSEX JCT.

VT 15

DAM

LIME KILN ROAD

AIRPORT

DAM

BURLINGTON

VT 116

VT 2A

US 7

I 89

RICHMOND   US 2

JONESVILLE

LAKE CHAMPLAIN

0   1   2   3 Miles

Arrow indicates direction of river flow.
Circle indicates breakpoint.

© 1999 The Countryman Press

north side of the river. Put in behind one of the old mill buildings at the Winooski Millyard access.

The railroad recrosses the river ½ mile below. The river starts a series of wide meanders around the edge of Burlington. The Winooski Valley Park District has established a number of picnic areas along the river: Muddy Brook (see above), Ethan Allen Homestead on the left 2½ miles from Winooski, and McCrea Farm farther down on the right. With advance permission camping may be possible. The VT 127 bridge crosses at mile 55¾. The last take-out is a fishing access farther downstream on the right side ¾ mile above the river's mouth at Lake Champlain (mi. 58½).

The gorge below the Mad River and the rapids, looking downstream

10

Lamoille River

Miles	Cumulative Miles	Breakpoints	River Rating	Special Difficulties
	0	Johnson		
8½			Q	
	8½	Jeffersonville		
12¼			Q	Dam*
	20¾	Fairfax Falls		
6½			1,2	
	27¼	Arrowhead Mountain Lake		
3½			F	Dam*
	30¾	Milton Dam		
3½			F,1	Dam*
	34¼	West Milton Dam		
5¾			F	
	40	Lake Champlain		
* Does not require portage if taking out at breakpoint.				

One of three big rivers that breaks through the main ridge of the Green Mountains, the Lamoille flows west across northern Vermont to enter Lake Champlain above Burlington. In its course, it passes through the second deepest trench in the Green Mountain range and then wends its way across

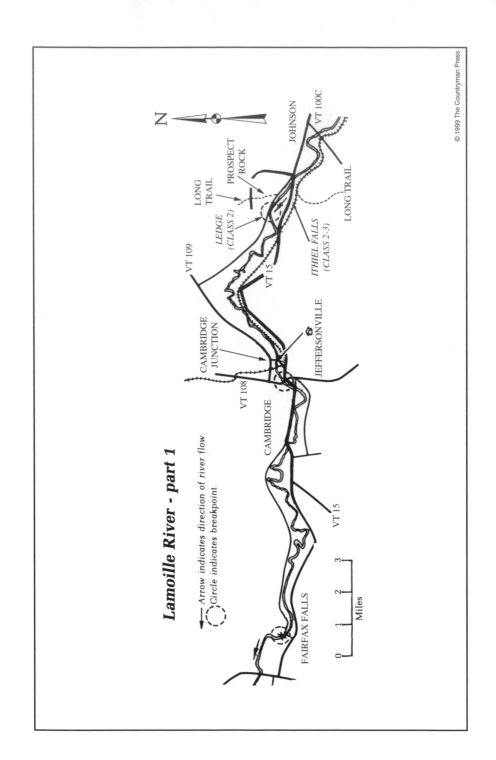

Lamoille River - part 1

Arrow indicates direction of river flow.
Circle indicates breakpoint.

FAIRFAX FALLS

Miles
0 1 2 3

VT 15

CAMBRIDGE

VT 108

CAMBRIDGE JUNCTION

VT 109

JEFFERSONVILLE

VT 15

LEDGE (CLASS 2)

LONG TRAIL

PROSPECT ROCK

ITHIEL FALLS (CLASS 2-3)

LONG TRAIL

JOHNSON

VT 100C

N

© 1999 The Countryman Press

Children enjoy breakfast more if they cook it themselves.

typical Vermont countryside. The Lamoille valley is wider than that of the Winooski, and its towns are smaller. The upper portion, where the river flows easily and quickly, is better for canoe camping, because the shorter flatwater stretches below Fairfax Falls are broken by two dams and rapids that require portages. Mountain views to both sides are excellent, and one of Vermont's two remaining covered railroad bridges spans the river east of Johnson, although not on the portion described here.

The Long Trail used to cross the Lamoille at the VT 15 bridge west of Johnson. With an elevation of only 500 feet, this is the trail's second lowest point. From the south the Long Trail has been relocated east off a road; a new shelter has been built, and a bridge will be built across the river to join the trail going north.

For an excellent view of the Lamoille Valley, hike north on the Long Trail, climbing steeply for ¾ mile to Prospect Rock. You can see the Sterling range to the south, but nearby peaks obscure Mount Mansfield 10 miles southwest. The road up the notch behind Prospect Rock is now drivable, so you may prefer to drive up while doing your car shuttle and walk an easier ¼ mile south.·

Shortly after passing the VT 15 bridge the river reaches a ledge with a 100-yard, class 2 rapid that is rocky in low water and has standing waves in high water. A mile farther on, Ithiel Falls is similar but somewhat more difficult, especially in high water.

Johnson to Jeffersonville (9 miles)

Most people will prefer to put in below these ledges. From the VT 15 bridge west of Johnson follow the road on the northern bank west for 1½ miles. Where the river comes close to the road again on the right bank, it divides to flow swiftly around several large granite islands. Put in here (mi. 0). Courtesy indicates that you should move your car to the second of the pull-offs uphill to the east after unloading, to clear the small parking area for other canoeists. Below this short stretch of fast water the Lamoille begins its leisurely meander across the valley floor. This is a very attractive section of river, and several outfitters run trips on it.

A covered bridge closed to vehicles crosses the river at Cambridge Junction (mi. 7¼), and VT 108 crosses at Jeffersonville (mi. 8½). Half a mile upstream of the bridge on VT 109, on the right, is a picnic area that offers difficult access and is used by the liveries. It may be easier to take out just downstream at a steep bank.

The best water-level take-out is at a ball field (with an industrial toilet) upstream on the left of the VT 15 bridge, a mile farther downstream. Between these two spots is an easy rapid—easy in medium water, when you can keep to the right over the gravel bar. In low water the only channel on the left is obstructed by overhanging trees and rocks, and could be dangerous to the unskillful.

Jeffersonville to Fairfax Falls (14½ miles)

Below the VT 15 bridge (mi. 9) the river continues to meander through pastoral countryside to Fairfax Falls; Mount Mansfield, Vermont's highest peak, is clearly visible to the southeast. At Cambridge (mi. 12) VT 15 again crosses the river.

To portage the dam at Fairfax Falls, take out above the bridge (mi. 22¾)—neither side is very easy—and carry downstream on the road on the right (north) side of the river for ¼ mile to a dirt track on the left. This turns sharply back upstream, leading down to the river (mi. 23).

Fairfax Falls to Arrowhead Mountain Lake (6½ miles)

Below the dam fast water continues for 2 miles to the VT 104 bridge at Fairfax (mi. 25). The short stretch of easy rapids below is followed by about 1 mile of flattish water. Around a bend in the river to the left, you begin to hear and then see the whitecaps of Two Islands Rapids. In medium water, these rapids are class 2 to 3 and should be inspected before you run them. Fast water and easy rapids extend for another 2 miles to Five Chutes. These chutes are formed by a transverse ledge and are class 2 in medium water. Each of them can be run, and canoe groups frequently spend a long time here trying them all. Of all the rapids along this stretch only Five Chutes can be scouted in advance; take a dirt road on the left bank, which you can approach from the East Georgia bridge.

It is ¼ mile from Five Chutes to the bridge at East Georgia and just beyond it lies Arrowhead Mountain Lake (mi. 32¾).

Trying out a prospective site for lumps before erecting the tent

Lamoille River - part 2

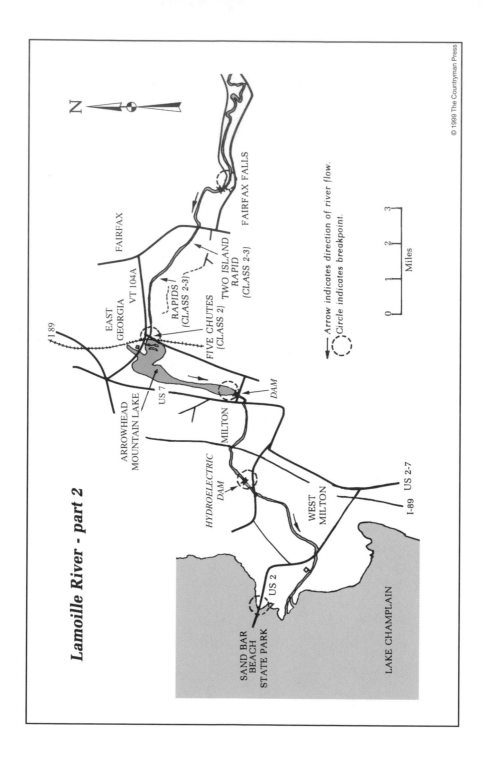

N

FAIRFAX

EAST
GEORGIA

FAIRFAX FALLS

VT 104A

RAPIDS
(CLASS 2-3)

TWO ISLAND
RAPID
(CLASS 2-3)

FIVE CHUTES
(CLASS 2)

I-189

ARROWHEAD
MOUNTAIN LAKE

US 7

DAM

MILTON

HYDROELECTRIC
DAM

WEST
MILTON

I-89   US 2-7

US 2

SAND BAR
BEACH
STATE PARK

LAKE CHAMPLAIN

Arrow indicates direction of river flow.

Circle indicates breakpoint.

0   1   2   3
Miles

© 1999 The Countryman Press

Arrowhead Mountain Lake to Milton Dam (3¾ miles)

Arrowhead Mountain Lake, formed by the Milton Dam, is shaped like a backward question mark. Put in or take out at a fishing access on the lake's northern end. A relatively small lake, its wider upper end is dotted with islands while the lower, southern end reaches into a narrow valley and is not much wider than the original river. Take out on either side above the dam (mi. 33¼).

Milton Dam to West Milton Dam (3¾ miles)

From Arrowhead Mountain Lake portage along the road for about 1 mile to the Milton Hydroelectric Station.

After 1 mile of fast water, you pass under I-89 and enter the backwater from the Peterson Hydroelectric Dam at West Milton. The remaining 1¾ miles to this dam are very wild and scenic. Be careful when approaching the dam (mi. 47); take out on the left bank past the last large ledge outcrop to portage. Carry along the power station access road as far as the town road, unless you want to run the 100 yards of class 3 rapids immediately below the dam.

West Milton Dam to Lake Champlain (5¾ miles)

The Lamoille has flatwater for its last 5½ miles to Lake Champlain. The West Milton bridge crosses ½ mile below the dam, and the Adirondacks across Lake Champlain are visible in the distance ahead. About 3 miles farther downstream you pass under US 2 (mi. 40½), the last access on the river is a short distance beyond. The mouth of the Lamoille is marshy, and the main channel meanders through a fair-sized delta.

Sand Bar Beach State Park on the lake lies 1½ miles north of the river and is a pleasant place to end your trip.

Missisquoi River

Miles	Cumulative Miles	Breakpoints	River Rating	Special Difficulties
	0	North Troy		
16			F,Q	
	16	East Richford		
18½			Γ,Q,1	2 rapids (class 2–3); dam washing out; dam*
	34½	Enosburg Falls		
11			F,Q,2	Dam*
	45½	Sheldon Springs		
0¼			F,Q,2	"Unrunnable" ledge; dam*
	53¾	Highgate Falls		
7			F,Q	Dam
	60¾	Swanton		
8			F,Q	
	68¾	Lake Champlain		
* Does not require portage if taking out at breakpoint.				

One of Vermont's northernmost rivers, the Missisquoi runs north along the eastern slopes of the Green Mountains into Quebec, where it loops through the range's northern foothills. Crossing back into Vermont, it flows

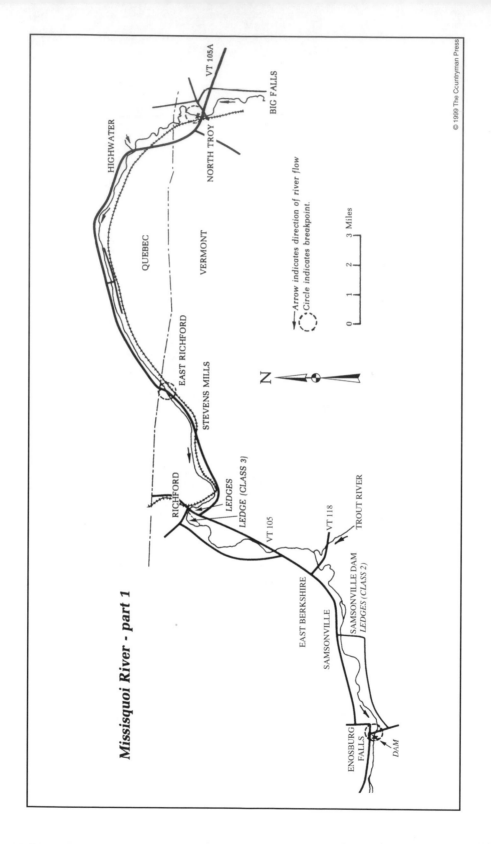

Missisquoi River - part 1

VT 105A

BIG FALLS

NORTH TROY

HIGHWATER

QUEBEC

VERMONT

EAST RICHFORD

STEVENS MILLS

Arrow indicates direction of river flow
Circle indicates breakpoint.

N

0   1   2   3 Miles

RICHFORD

LEDGES

LEDGE (CLASS 3)

VT 105

VT 118

TROUT RIVER

EAST BERKSHIRE

SAMSONVILLE

SAMSONVILLE DAM
LEDGES (CLASS 2)

ENOSBURG
FALLS

DAM

west to drain into Missisquoi Bay at the northern end of Lake Champlain. The river passes only small towns, and most local mills no longer discharge wastes into the river, so its waters are fairly clean.

Downstream from North Troy the river alternates between fast current and smooth water broken by occasional rapids and dams. Only four of the largest dams once built below North Troy remain intact. These do not affect canoeing, since natural waterfalls at these sites would have to be portaged anyway.

Just before reaching North Troy the Missisquoi passes through Big Falls, a splendid gorge that merits a side trip. To see it, drive 2 miles south from North Troy on River Road along the eastern bank. The river undercuts a 50-foot cliff, and the upper cascades ¼ mile above the falls have some interesting eroded ledges and potholes.

North Troy to East Richford (16 miles)

North Troy is just south of the Canadian border on VT 105. Before unloading, drive 1½ miles north on VT 105A and report to Canadian Customs.

The hardest part of the stretch is putting in below the North Troy Dam. A devious route through the mill yard and across the railroad tracks goes along the right bank to the river. You can also put in from a farm off Pine Street on the right bank, 1 mile farther downstream. This spot is better in dry weather, since you must negotiate a dirt track ½ mile long before you reach the river. The section from North Troy to Highwater was reported to be blocked by trees in 1998. Check locally.

Beware when asking directions to a good put-in; some townsfolk think "below the dam" means to the south and may direct you to the nice landing off River Road—which unfortunately is upstream of the dam.

Across the border in Quebec, the Missisquoi seems not to cut through the mountains but to outflank them. Should you wish to start in Highwater, go north from the bridge on Route 243 for 2 miles and put in on the North Branch, which is easier and has better parking. The confluence is within sight of the bridge in Highwater. Below Highwater (mi. 5¾) in Quebec the volume of the river is much larger and fallen trees less of a problem. The river meanders through a fairly broad valley with farmland broken by patches of woodland. Shortly after the first bridge an RV campground (mi. 6) fronts the river on the right. Where a side road crosses in another 6 miles, the Missisquoi curves southwest and flows back into Vermont.

Heed the sign at the high bridge in East Richford (mi. 16) and land on the left to report to American Customs just at the top of the bank.

East Richford to Enosburg Falls (18½ miles)

The first 5 miles from East Richford to Richford (mi. 21) are predominantly class 1 water. Numerous islands create networks of channels and intricate bifurcations; the banks are very wild and scenic, but careful water reading is necessary to pick out the best channels.

Watch for a railroad bridge crossing the Missisquoi 1¼ miles above Richford. Shortly afterward, the river comes close to the road; this is a possible take-out if you do not wish to run the rapids that start in town just below a factory on the left bank. For the length of the rapids in Richford, the river is contained within sheer bridge abutments and high retaining walls and is impeded with transverse ledges; since you can easily see the rapids from the Richford bridge, it is best to scout them in advance to plan a course of action. Just downstream of the bridge a river-level gauge is painted on a building on the left; we found 1½ feet a good height to run the river. The class 2 ledges above the Richford bridge should be run well on the left. The rapids continue below the bridge, increase in intensity, and culminate in a big drop over a class 3 ledge. A clear but narrow channel runs down to the left of center through large standing waves. The town park on the right offers access or a preview.

Slower current, occasional riffles, some flatwater, and impressive mountain views characterize the run below Richford to Samsonville (mi. 30). To the left rise the Green Mountains' northern peaks; to the right, the lower, more rounded hills along the international border. The old railroad bed is now an All Season Recreational Trail, no motor vehicles allowed, used mostly by bikers and an occasional walker during the canoeing season.

The railroad and VT 105 bridges (mi. 25¾) cross together 5 miles below Richford. Trout River enters on the left 1½ miles downstream. It is often paddled down from Montgomery, with a fast current and many meanders. Half a mile below, VT 118 crosses at East Berkshire (mi. 27¾).

Parts of the old Samsonville Dam (mi. 29¾) still stand in the middle of the river 2 miles below the VT 118 bridge. You can see the dam and the ledges below it from VT 105. The dam is breached on the left as well as the right. Most people find it easier to portage or line on the left. Only those who

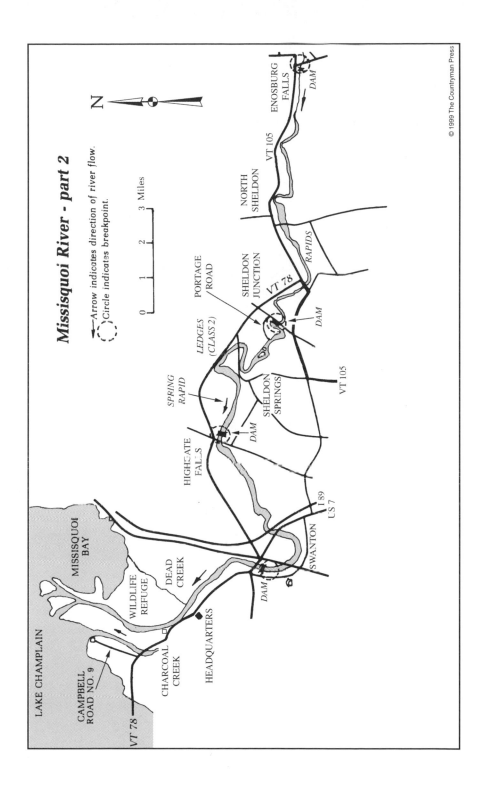

Missisquoi River - part 2

Arrow indicates direction of river flow.
Circle indicates breakpoint.

0   1   2   3 Miles

N

LAKE CHAMPLAIN

MISSISQUOI BAY

WILDLIFE REFUGE

CAMPBELL ROAD NO. 9

VT 78

CHARCOAL CREEK

DEAD CREEK

HEADQUARTERS

DAM

SWANTON

I 89

US 7

VT 105

SHELDON SPRINGS

HIGHGATE FALLS

DAM

SPRING RAPID

LEDGES (CLASS 2)

PORTAGE ROAD

SHELDON JUNCTION

VT 78

DAM

RAPIDS

NORTH SHELDON

VT 105

ENOSBURG FALLS

DAM

thought the Richford drop was easy should land on the right to look this ledge over before running it. It has a considerable hydraulic and should be scouted carefully; spikes have caused problems in low water. Since the dam is washing out, conditions will change after each storm. Class 2 ledges immediately below continue for about ½ mile and can be run in several places.

A little over 1 mile below the Samsonville Dam you pass under the North Enosburg bridge (mi. 31); smooth water continues to Enosburg Falls (mi. 34½). Land above the bridge on the left to portage the dam.

If you wish to run the half mile of class 2–3 rapids below the dam, portage on the left down the hill to a suitable relaunching spot. The rapids are easy at the start, but around the corner drop through heavy waves at an old dam site.

The longer portage, ½ mile, is on the right. Go north on VT 108, turn left on St. Albans Street, and continue on to the fire lane on the left.

Enosburg Falls to Sheldon Springs (11 miles)

The water remains smooth for another 6 miles to the North Sheldon bridge (mi. 40¾). The 3 miles of rapids between the bridges at North Sheldon and Sheldon Junction (mi. 43¼) are scratchy or impossible in very low water. The river flows gently again for the remaining 2 miles to Sheldon Springs. Take out on the right above the bridge (mi. 45⅛) to portage the dam below. No take-out is marked.

Sheldon Springs to Highgate Falls (8¼ miles)

An extensive cascade drops below the newly rebuilt dam. The access on the left is for heavy-water enthusiasts with expert canoeing skills, who have scouted it carefully.

Start the portage to the foot of the rapids by turning right on Shawville Road. Take the second gate to the left in ⅒ mile; it is marked by large SHELDON SPRINGS HYDROELECTRIC PROJECT signs. Follow the paved road uphill, then down a steep hill to the power station. The total portage is 1⅓ miles. You may drive your car down this road to unload. Get permission before parking.

The water level in this and in the subsequent section of the river may fluctuate drastically when the gates are opened and closed for power generation.

You can run the rapid's lower end if you wish. Below, the river continues for a pleasant 3-mile paddle. This stretch was seldom run in the past because the plywood and wood products mill at Sheldon Springs discharged effluent and bark chips here. The plant has cleaned up its operation, and no signs of earlier pollution remain.

A stretch of rapids and class 2 ledges begins just above the bridge in East Highgate (mi. 49½), you can scout this in advance from either the bridge or VT 78 on the right bank. These ledges have shallow spots and sharp drops that require careful planning, and the abutments of an old dam, in the process of being undermined, still stand just below the bridge. The rapids continue for ½ mile, with their entire length visible from the road.

Below the rapids, the Missisquoi again leaves the highway. One mile above Highgate Falls, you begin to hear the river roar as it rushes through two ledges ⅒ mile apart. Unfortunately, you cannot conveniently scout these ledges in advance. Although the first can be run, the second drops 5 feet and is unrunnable over the main drop for all but the suicidal ledge enthusiast. However, a strong, skillful paddler can land on the right just above the second for an easy carry. Those who miss this landing will regret it. You

Lining the ledges below the Samsonville dam

The fisherboys on the rock enjoyed watching the canoes pass by. The railroad bridge above Richford is in the background.

may choose to begin your carry farther upstream on the right. If you are lining, work on the left where the drop is more even and the river more shallow. You can also line the main drop on the left.

This set of ledges is called Spring Rapid, in reference to a mineral spring in the woods high to your left. Water from the spring was once bottled and sold for medicinal purposes.

Below the ledges the river broadens into a pond behind the dam at Highgate Falls (mi. 53¾). The dam lies above an old iron bridge that replaced one of Vermont's earliest covered bridges and was recently designated a historic landmark. A new bridge is around the corner downstream. The carry is shorter on the left, but you can drive to the northern end of the closed bridge on Mill Hill Road. Carry on the road across VT 207 and down to the power station.

Like many of Vermont's dams, the dam at Highgate Falls is one of a series that has occupied the site. The first dam at Highgate Falls was built in 1807 to drive a waterwheel, which generated power for a sawmill; after a few years of operation it was washed downstream by spring ice and high water.

The Keyes family, who at the time owned a good share of Highgate, rebuilt it to power a gristmill. A generating plant added later furnished the surrounding area with electrical power; this plant was eventually sold to the village of Swanton, which in turn built a new dam. Portions of the old wooden dam are still in place behind the present structure.

Highgate Falls to Swanton (7 miles)

Below the dam and around the bend, the river broadens into a large pool dotted with islands. Smooth water continues to Swanton (mi. 61). Three bridges cross the Missisquoi on this stretch: the I-89 bridge (mi. 57½), the US 7 bridge (mi. 57¾), and an old covered railroad bridge (mi. 60½). The latter, now abandoned, is one of only two covered railroad bridges still standing in Vermont. (The other, still in use, crosses the Lamoille east of Johnson.) Take out on either side above the Swanton Dam, which lies above the VT 78 bridge (mi. 60¾).

Swanton to Lake Champlain (8 miles)

Below Swanton the river is essentially lake travel. The first stretch runs parallel to VT 78, and backyards of several homes extend to the riverbank. Dead Creek, a side stream of the Missisquoi delta, branches off from the river opposite the Missisquoi Wildlife Refuge Headquarters (mi. 63¾). There is no access at the headquarters.

Dead Creek itself is attractive, and the area around it abounds in wildlife. Since fewer powerboats use this channel, you may prefer it as your route to the lake. The water is shallow with much vegetation and lies farther east than the map would imply. Paddle a short distance east across the bay to take out at the small resort town of Highgate Springs.

An alternate take-out is the boat-launching ramp (mi. 64¼) on the Missisquoi 1 mile below the Dead Creek junction. The river below here is well traveled by motorboats going to or from Lake Champlain (mi. 68¾).

A third possible take-out is a marina on the lake 1½ miles southwest (left) on the river mouth. It is situated on a point west of a blind channel called Charcoal Creek; you can reach it by car from Campbell Road 9, which follows Charcoal Creek.

Connecticut River
(West Stewartstown to Gilman)

Miles	Cumulative Miles	Breakpoints	River Rating	Special Difficulties
	0	West Stewartstown		
15			F,Q,1	
	15	Columbia		
9½			Q,1,2	Old dam
	24½	North Stratford		
11¼			Q	
	35¾	Stratford		
12¼			F,Q	Old dam*
	48½	Guildhall, Vermont		
20½			F,Q,1	Dam*
	69	Gilman Dam		

* Does not require portage if taking out at breakpoint.

The Connecticut River watershed forms the northern boundary between New Hampshire and Quebec, and farther downstream the river itself divides Vermont and New Hampshire before crossing into Massachusetts. Since the state line is fixed at the low-water mark on the Vermont shore, the upper Connecticut is actually in New Hampshire and is that state's longest river.

A long river with a moderate current and easy rapids, the Connecticut

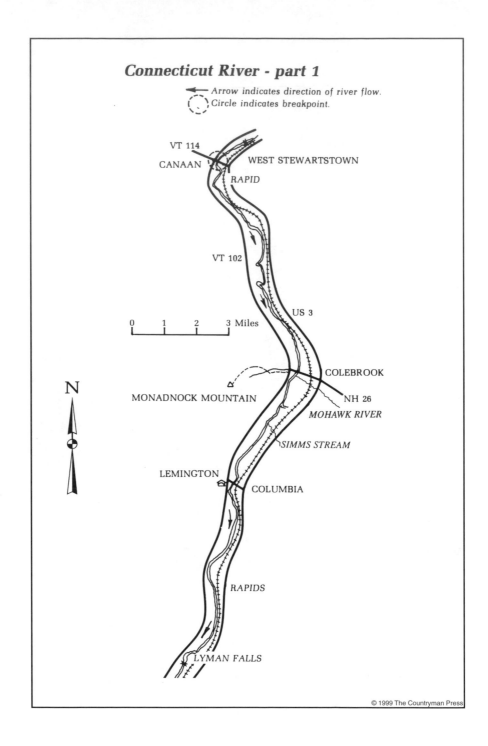

Connecticut River - part 1

← Arrow indicates direction of river flow.
◯ Circle indicates breakpoint.

VT 114

CANAAN   WEST STEWARTSTOWN

RAPID

VT 102

0   1   2   3 Miles

US 3

N

COLEBROOK

MONADNOCK MOUNTAIN   NH 26

MOHAWK RIVER

SIMMS STREAM

LEMINGTON

COLUMBIA

RAPIDS

LYMAN FALLS

© 1999 The Countryman Press

is very popular for canoeing, despite the aura of civilization and occasional dams. The 69-mile stretch from West Stewartstown near Quebec to Gilman contains some of the faster water on the Connecticut, although the river is mostly smooth. Only one long stretch of rapids and one old dam require special attention.

The Connecticut's drainage basin covers extensive timberland. This long river was an obvious choice for transporting logs to lumber mills farther downstream, and log drives were once an annual event. Today you can still find evidence of this earlier use along the river.

Before a log drive, cut logs were piled along the riverbanks in rollways. When the drive was ready to begin, the stakes holding these piles were removed—a very dangerous proceeding, since on occasion the whole pile would suddenly collapse and flatten whatever or whomever was in the way. Because a successful drive required an exact amount of water, small dams that could be blown out easily were built on the tributaries.

The rivermen had to keep the logs moving. Crews and teams of horses along both shores followed waist-deep in icy water to push stranded logs back into the current. Occasionally rapids were blasted apart to release or

The remains of a log crib that has been nearly washed out.

prevent big jams, and loggers had a running feud with owners of small mill-dams along the way.

Log booms (long lines of log chained together) also directed the floating timber. Strung across a blind eddy, they prevented swirling jams; fanned out above a dam, they guided the logs into a sluice; and stretched across a quiet part of the river by a mill, they brought the log drive to an end. Cables on trees or rings in the rock held the booms. When a needed natural anchorage did not exist, a log crib was manufactured. A cube of heavy timbers was laid up log-cabin style and filled with rocks and dirt to create an artificial island. These were built to withstand great pressure, and remains of many can still be seen.

During the big log drives everything from sawlogs to huge cook rafts ran the river. Rivermen on sawlogs could move from one log to another, paddling with a peavey or, in shallow water, poling with a pike pole. They could also move ahead by jumping violently down on one end, or sideways by rolling it.

The boat that loggers favored was a bateau. Its narrow bottom enabled it to spin easily, and its long, raking overhang and flared sides helped it slide over obstructions and float heavy loads in shallow water. Bateaux could run rocky rapids and heavy white water better than any other workboat and could be handled with oars, paddles, or poles.

A cook shack mounted on a huge raft often accompanied the crew and logs down the river. These cook rafts could run the dam at Guildhall and many big rapids, but at particularly high dams they had to be dismantled and reassembled below. (The large Comerford and Moore Dams, which inundated the Fifteen Mile Falls section of rapids downstream of the portion described here, were not built until after the last of the log drives.)

West Stewartstown to Columbia (15 miles)

The usual start for a trip on the upper Connecticut is the Vermont end of the Canaan–West Stewartstown bridge, off US 3 and near the junction of VT 102 and VT 114. A sign marking the 45th parallel of latitude is ½ mile north on US 3. The river here has few rocks and can usually be run even in very low water with a little wading in riffles; dams upstream control the water level.

Just beyond the first corner to the left, the river divides around two long,

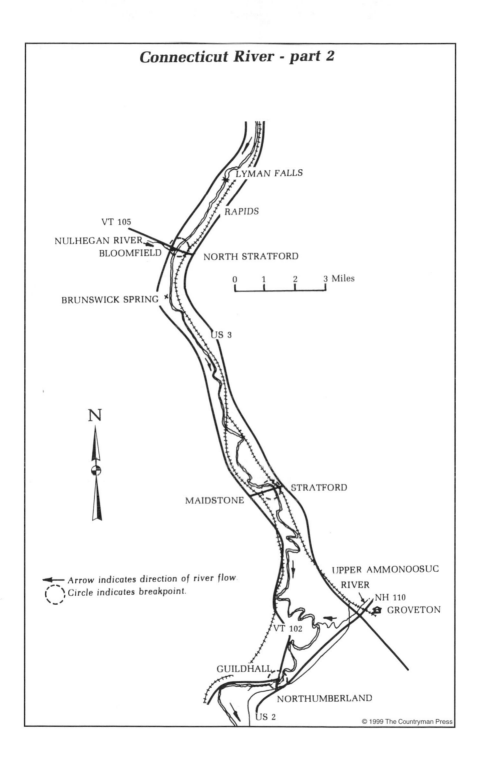

Connecticut River - part 2

LYMAN FALLS

RAPIDS

VT 105

NULHEGAN RIVER
BLOOMFIELD

NORTH STRATFORD

0 1 2 3 Miles

BRUNSWICK SPRING

US 3

N

STRATFORD

MAIDSTONE

UPPER AMMONOOSUC
RIVER

NH 110

GROVETON

Arrow indicates direction of river flow.
Circle indicates breakpoint.

VT 102

GUILDHALL

NORTHUMBERLAND

US 2

thin islands into three channels of runnable rapids. As in all narrow spots and fast corners, watch for obstructing trees. The river flows slowly to Colebrook, passing through a beautiful valley with woods and low-lying farmland close to the banks. Roads follow along both sides, but not closely.

When the river circles around to the left, Vermont's Monadnock Mountain becomes conspicuous ahead on the right. A trail up the mountain starts near the Colebrook bridge (mi. 10¼).

To climb Monadnock, land on the right downstream from the bridge. From telephone pole #NETT 81 PSCO 14, go up a farm lane between two houses, crawl under the gate, continue through the horse pasture, and cross the brook. A woods road follows the right bank of this brook upstream and degenerates into a trail. In-season the wildflowers are beautiful. After 1 mile the trail crosses to the left bank above a waterfall and then continues for another 1½ miles up through a forest of small evergreens to the summit. The old fire tower is in disrepair, a scenic attraction rather than a viewpoint.

Below Colebrook the current picks up and smooth water alternates with easy rapids to the covered Columbia Bridge (mi. 15).

Columbia to North Stratford (9½ miles)

Below Columbia the river continues to flow smoothly for about 2 more miles. It then enters a long stretch of class 2 rapids, which continue intermittently over the next 7½ miles to the Bloomfield–North Stratford bridge. In low water these rapids are too rocky to run. VT 102 comes close to the river where the rapids begin, so you can easily scout the first stretch in advance or take out if necessary.

About 5 miles from the onset of rapids, the old Lyman Falls Dam (mi. 22½) is exceedingly difficult to spot from above, and in high water canoes are frequently swept over it by mistake. Rocks on the left-hand side at a right-hand turn where the rapids start warn you. As you round a gentle left-hand turn where the river is wide with a side channel cutting left and a steep bank on the right, watch for it. A small abutment and piece of the dam are on the right. The dam is breached on both sides; the New Hampshire side may be easier to land and/or line. Even at suitable water levels, many people choose not to run this spot because of the spikes and jagged blocks that remain from the old dam. With difficulty you can inspect the dam in advance from VT 102, ¼ mile downstream from the Vermont Highway Department garage.

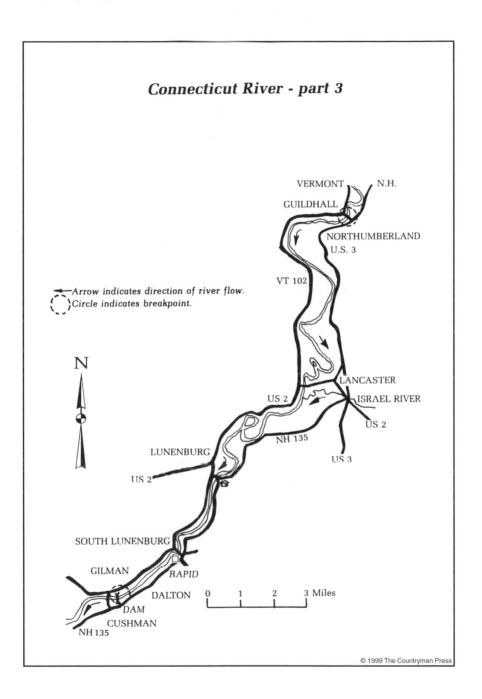

Connecticut River - part 3

Arrow indicates direction of river flow.
Circle indicates breakpoint.

VERMONT   N.H.

GUILDHALL

NORTHUMBERLAND
U.S. 3

VT 102

N

LANCASTER

US 2   ISRAEL RIVER

US 2

NH 135

US 3

LUNENBURG

US 2

SOUTH LUNENBURG

GILMAN   RAPID

DALTON   0   1   2   3 Miles

DAM
CUSHMAN
NH 135

© 1999 The Countryman Press

Beyond the dam the rapids become easier as you approach the Bloom-field–North Stratford bridge (mi. 24½).

North Stratford to Stratford (11¼ miles)

There are no rapids below North Stratford, and the river again runs smoothly for the next 11¼ miles. A rapid called the Horserace was mistakenly located here in some earlier guidebooks. Different sources place this rapid in different locations, but all the spots mentioned are now inundated by the backwater of the Comerford and Moore Dams and are all well downstream of Gilman, the final take-out on this portion of the Connecticut.

About 1½ miles from the North Stratford bridge and just upstream of a high cliff on the right, a distinctive brownish stain in the water marks the Brunswick Mineral Spring location (mi. 26). An old hotel catering to those who came for the spring's mineral waters once stood above this spot.

Past the cliff the river winds through farmland and pasture to the Maidstone-Stratford bridge (mi. 35¾), above which you can take out on the right.

Stratford to Guildhall (12¾ miles)

The river continues to wander placidly down the valley to Guildhall, still uninterrupted by rapids. The Upper Ammonoosuc River (mi. 45¾), which enters on the left 10 miles below Stratford, used to bring polluted water from the mills at Groveton. Now the water is treated, and this greatly improves the run downstream. You can see the Percy Peaks, a pair of sharp, pointed mountains in New Hampshire, here on the left. About 3 miles farther and just below the bridge is the old Wyoming Dam at Guildhall (mi. 48½). Take out above the bridge on either side.

Guildhall to Gilman Dam (20½ miles)

The old dam at Guildhall is pretty well washed out. This section features some well-preserved log cribs and other logging remains. The countryside is rural; the meanders are very deep, with attractive sandbars. The US 2 bridge is 9¼ miles downstream, and the Lancaster covered bridge another 5¾. Below the railroad bridge in South Lunenburg (mi. 66½) on the left is a good boat access at the junction of NH 142 and 135. Below this is a class 1 rapid with boulders in the middle and on the left. Keep right.

The portage trail at Gilman Dam (mi. 69) starts in a deep bay on the left above the log boom, leading to a gravel road where a car may be driven. This road is now gated; you can borrow the key from security (open 24 hours) at the gate of the Simpson Paper Company at the Vermont end of the dam just upstream of the bridge at Monroe. You do not need a key to hand-carry past the dam. It may be easier to avoid this problem by using the water-level ramp 2½ miles upstream.

Below the dam the river comes into the ponding from Moore Reservoir.

13

Connecticut River
(Comerford Dam to Orford)

Miles	Cumulative Miles	Breakpoints	River Rating	Special Difficulties
	0	Comerford Dam		
6¾			Q,1	Dam*
	6¾	McIndoe Falls		
8¼			F,Q,1,2	Dam
	15	Woodsville		
10½			Q	
	25½	Newbury		
18			F	
	43½	Orford		
* Does not require portage if taking out at breakpoint.				

The Connecticut River from Comerford Dam, west of Littleton, New Hampshire, to Orford is fairly large and can be run anytime, although occasional shallow spots may appear in the wider expanses. The river is mostly quickwater along this 43-mile stretch, with a few riffles and easy rapids and two large dams that require portages. The stretch from Newbury to Wilder Dam, 20 miles below Orford, is especially popular; there are several campgrounds, picnic areas, and launching ramps between Orford and Wilder Dam. Current information on water flow and campsites in this area is available at the visitors information center at either Moore Dam (upstream of

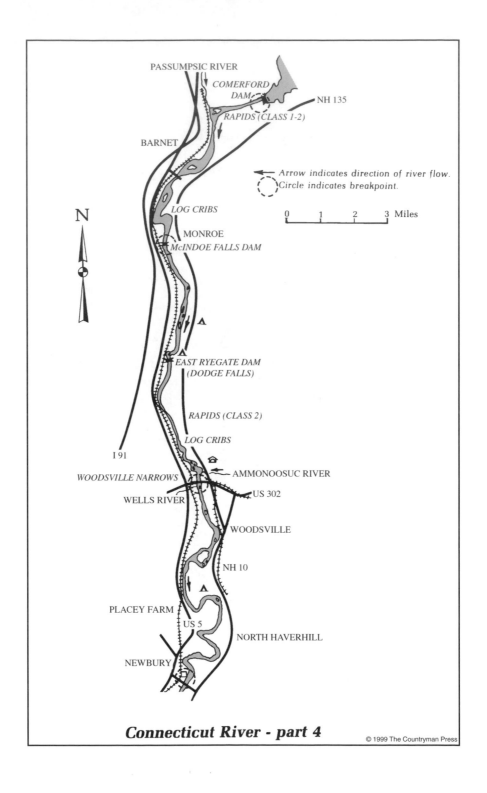

PASSUMPSIC RIVER

COMERFORD
DAM
NH 135

RAPIDS (CLASS 1-2)

BARNET

← Arrow indicates direction of river flow.
◯ Circle indicates breakpoint.

N

LOG CRIBS

0   1   2   3 Miles

MONROE
McINDOE FALLS DAM

Λ

Λ
EAST RYEGATE DAM
(DODGE FALLS)

RAPIDS (CLASS 2)

LOG CRIBS

I 91

WOODSVILLE NARROWS   AMMONOOSUC RIVER
WELLS RIVER   US 302

WOODSVILLE

NH 10

Λ
PLACEY FARM
US 5   NORTH HAVERHILL

NEWBURY

Connecticut River - part 4

© 1999 The Countryman Press

Comerford Dam) or Wilder Dam (below Hanover). Both centers are in New Hampshire.

The Upper Valley Land Trust has arranged for 19 campsites (as of fall 1998) on the following section of the Connecticut River. For a current list of all the campsites on the upper Connecticut River contact the Upper Valley Land Trust, 19 Buck Road, Hanover, NH 03775 (603-643-6626). Relevant campsites are described in the text; numbers in parentheses are the land trust's campsite numbers.

Comerford Dam to McIndoe Falls (6¾ miles)

Comerford Dam can only be reached from the New Hampshire side of the river off NH 135. A picnic area with an outstanding view upstream is provided. Unfortunately, access below the dam is rather tedious. Carry down the grassy slope adjacent to the dam, slide down a steep, rocky incline, and continue downstream through rocks and mud another ⅒ mile to a launching spot. At least it's mostly downhill.

The water level fluctuates drastically as the dam opens and closes, and water can wash down the river below in a mini tidal wave inches high when the dam is opened. We were once cooling off after a carry with a swim when one such wave suddenly descended and thoroughly soaked our clothes, which we had folded neatly on a flat rock beside the water. The canoe was afloat by the time we salvaged our clothes; fortunately, following our usual custom, we had tied it securely. The water level quickly rose another 2 feet.

The water along this stretch runs fast, with riffles and some turbulence. The Passumpsic River (mi. 1½) joins the Connecticut 1½ miles below the dam. Paddle an easy half mile up the Passumpsic to see a pretty gorge just below the last dam on that river. An easy rapid lies by the river mouth and riffles continue below it. According to local anglers, the deep pools interspersed among these riffles hide lunkers. Below, the river flows more quickly around some small islands.

Land on the left above the Monroe bridge to portage the McIndoe Falls Dam just below (mi. 6¾). The bank here is steep and muddy. Carry less than ¼ mile across the paved road and down a dirt track to a sandy cove. McIndoe Falls Dam gives anglers and canoeists below a sporting chance by sounding a horn when the gates are opened.

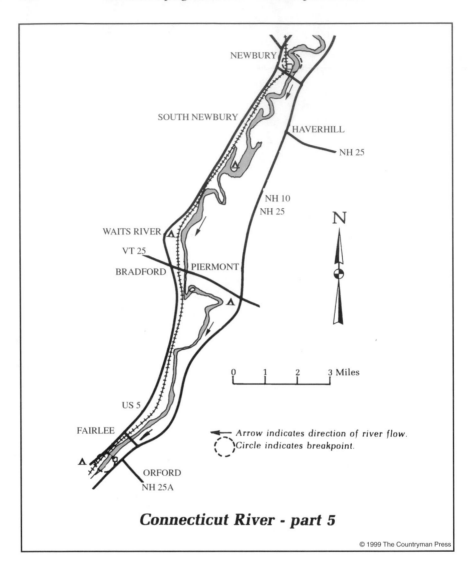

Connecticut River - part 5

© 1999 The Countryman Press

McIndoe Falls to Woodsville (8¼ miles)

Fast water continues 4 miles to the dam at Dodge Falls (East Ryegate, mi. 10¾). Fiddlehead Island Campsite (#1A, mi. 9¾) is on the third of three wooded islands. A conspicuously sharp bend to the left precedes the dam, and a factory rises from the right bank just below the dam. Dodge Falls Campsite (#1), with two lean-tos in a pine grove, is located on the portage trail on the left (New Hampshire) side. Access to this by road is from NH 135, where an inconspicuous sign—DODGE FALLS HYDRO—marks what looks like a farm lane. Downstream access is also possible on the Vermont side.

Below the dam the river widens and has some shallow spots. After 3 miles you reach Woodsville Narrows (mi. 13¾), notable for its sharp S curves and narrow passes through high cliffs. Rapids run the length of the narrows; beyond them, whirlpools create some turbulence in the broad pool just above the mouth of the Ammonoosuc River. For those starting in Woodsville, there is access at the southern end of the recreation field half a mile downstream of the bridge on NH 135. The Wells River, where there is also access, enters on the right a short distance downstream (mi. 15).

Woodsville was once the head of navigation on the Connecticut, with canals and locks circumventing dams and rapids downstream. Early commercial vessels were flatboats that were sailed up the river when there was enough wind and poled up when there was not. After steamboats were introduced to the river, attempts to venture farther upstream to Barnet, Vermont (above McIndoe Falls), followed, and the *Barnet* was built specifically for the run. Unfortunately, her designers neglected to check the dimensions of the locks around the Bellows Falls rapids; the *Barnet* didn't fit and was forced to retire downstream in ignominy. The advent of railroads ended commercial navigation on the Connecticut.

Woodsville to Newbury (10½ miles)

Fast riffles continue below the high Woodsville bridge for ½ mile. Two miles below Woodsville is the Howard Island Campsite (#1B). Land on a rocky beach just west of the berm that connects it to the NH shore; camp on the edge of the field above. Smooth water with a fair current and some shallow spots in low water follows as the river winds to Newbury. The Placey Farm (mi. 18), visible from US 5, its name conspicuous in large white letters on a red barn, marks the beginning of backwater from Wilder Dam 45 miles south. The river gradually becomes slower and deeper, although the valley is so steep that the lake formed by the dam is not noticeable. A launching ramp on the right upstream of the Newbury bridge (mi. 25½) offers a possible take-out.

Much of the Connecticut River along this stretch runs through land still dedicated to farming.

Newbury to Orford (18 miles)

The covered bridge connecting South Newbury to Haverhill collapsed just after it had been refurbished and made into a New Hampshire state park. Access is possible but not particularly good from the New Hampshire side. A mile below the park is Vaughan Meadows Campsite (#3, mi. 30), on a wooded bank after the river turns from southeast to south, a few hundred yards north of the Bradford line. The river continues its slow and circuitous course past the Waits River mouth (mi. 34¾). A short paddle up the Waits River is Bugbee Landing Campsite (#4) at the public boat ramp, near water, toilets, and stores. Below the Bradford bridge (mi. 36) the Underhill Campsite (#5, mi. 37) appears after the river turns sharply northeast, then swings east-southeast with Piermont village ahead. The campsite is on a point of land on the left immediately above Eastman Brook, just before the river turns sharply southwest.

Orford (mi. 43) is scenic, with cliffs rising above the bridge. You may take out on the left at the launching ramp (mi. 43½) ½ mile below the Orford bridge or continue downstream to the many campgrounds, picnic areas, and launching ramps along the 20-mile stretch to Wilder Dam.

14

White River–Connecticut River

Miles	Cumulative Miles	Breakpoints	River Rating	Special Difficulties
		White River		
	0	Granville		
7¼			1	
	7¼	Lions Park		
9½			Q,1,2	
	16¾	Stockbridge		
9			2	
	25¾	Bethel		
11¾			Q,1	Occasional ledges (class 2)
	37½	Sharon		
6¼			2	Old dam
	43¾	West Hartford		
7¼			Q,1	Ledge
	51	Connecticut River		
7¾			Q,1	Falls*
	58¾	Sumner Falls		

* Does not require portage if taking out at breakpoint.

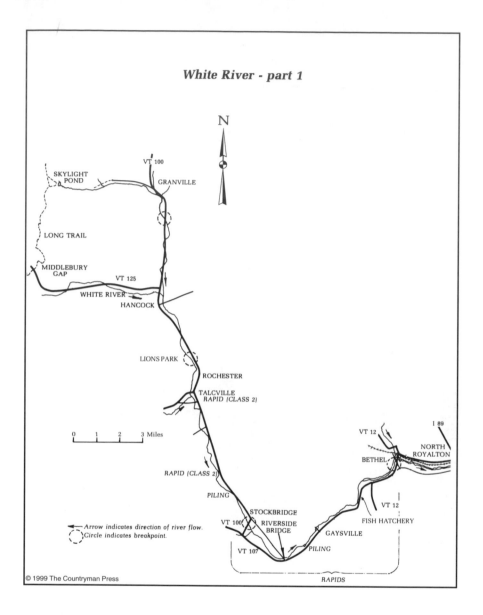

White River - part 1

N

VT 100

SKYLIGHT POND

GRANVILLE

LONG TRAIL

MIDDLEBURY GAP

VT 125

WHITE RIVER

HANCOCK

LIONS PARK

ROCHESTER

TALCVILLE
RAPID (CLASS 2)

0   1   2   3 Miles

RAPID (CLASS 2)

PILING

VT 12

NORTH ROYALTON

I 89

BETHEL

STOCKBRIDGE

VT 100

RIVERSIDE BRIDGE

GAYSVILLE

VT 12

FISH HATCHERY

Arrow indicates direction of river flow.
Circle indicates breakpoint.

VT 107

PILING

RAPIDS

The White River, in combination with the Winooski and its tributary the Mad River, was a main Indian route between lower New England and Montreal. However, it was the easy travel through the valley to the lower mountain passes rather than the river itself that made this a well-traveled route. The White is a rocky river with a quick current, and along its upper reaches can only be run during high or medium water. Although it is not extremely difficult and is popular with canoeing groups, the White is the most demanding river described in this guidebook.

The upper river is best run in May when the water level is high or after a heavy rain. The river below Bethel can be run in a moderately wet summer but not in very dry weather. Its clear water and pools invite swimming, and its pleasantly fast current makes this a good river to use as practice for white-water canoe camping trips. You get the feeling of handling a loaded boat in a current in the easy water at the start below the Lions Park, while the rapids below Stockbridge require considerable maneuvering skill. Some of the riffles below Bethel require good water reading, and the ledges give

Wading a canoe down a shallow riffle

you a chance to run through high waves. Roads along the river offer refuge in case of an accident.

The White River rises in Skylight Pond, a beautiful little spot that can be reached by a 5-mile hike north on the Long Trail from VT 125 in Middlebury Gap. Once my daughter and I followed the river from Skylight Pond, where it leaves as a tiny trickle, to its confluence with the Connecticut at White River Junction. For its first 2 miles, it splashes over rocks and under moss down the side of the mountain. A drivable dirt road follows it down the next 3 miles to Granville, where it becomes navigable near the first VT 100 bridge.

From this point, the river offers 51 miles of almost unobstructed canoeing to the Connecticut at White River Junction, with another 7¾ unimpeded miles down the Connecticut to Sumner Falls. This is the longest almost continuously rapid run without a carry in the area.

White River

Granville to Lions Park (7¼ miles)

This 7¼-mile stretch is runnable in high water only. Put in where VT 100 crosses the White just below Granville. Here the river is small with a fast current and is sometimes obstructed by fallen trees.

VT 100 crosses three times along this stretch. The river also passes beneath a side-road bridge below Hancock (mi. 4¼) and there is a new access at the next VT 100 bridge, 1½ miles north of Rochester.

Lions Park to Stockbridge (9½ miles)

Lions Park (mi. 7¼), on the left bank about 1 mile above Rochester on VT 100, is the usual put-in for a run down the upper portion of the White. The VT 73 bridge crosses 1½ miles from the park, and ½ mile below, the West Branch entering from the right almost doubles the river's size.

A class 2 rapid runs above and below the Talcville bridge (mi. 9½) and is easily seen from the bridge and from VT 100. The river then curves in leisurely fashion through a cow pasture, where it scatters around several sandy islands.

After 3 miles of easy going, the river turns right and divides around another island. Land on the left bank beside the island to scout a class 2 rapid (mi. 12¾), which lies beneath a high bank where the two channels rejoin and the river bends to the left. Below the rapid the river again flows easily as far as Stockbridge (mi. 16¾).

Stockbridge to Bethel (9 miles)

One of the more difficult stretches of rapids runs from Stockbridge to Gaysville. These rapids run class 2 in medium water and up to class 3 in high water, with eddies and considerable waves. In places the river is wide, and in medium water the current sifts evenly among the rocks, challenging your water-reading skills. You cannot run this stretch in low water.

Waves on the outside corner under the Riverside bridge (mi. 19½), 2¾ miles below Stockbridge, can swamp or upset a canoe. One mile farther downstream an old bridge piling lies in the middle of the river (mi. 20½); it can be run on the right in high water, or on the left, but not through the middle, although indecisive canoeists occasionally try.

Dodging rocks is a major feature of running rapids in Vermont.

Where VT 107 climbs high on the right and the river swings left, the water drops through some big rocks with high standing waves. A pool lies below and a picnic area sits high up the bank on the right. Beyond the pool and around the corner, the river passes over an awkward ledge that you can scout in advance from the picnic area. This rapid has changed considerably during the past 30 years; the river rearranges the rocks with each storm.

As the river approaches the high cliff at Gaysville, it swings left through another fast outside corner with standing waves. A privately owned campground fronts the river's right bank just below the bridge in Gaysville.

Beyond Gaysville the rapids become less continuous, although two steep ledges about ½ mile apart not far from Gaysville and clearly visible from VT 107 still require attention. A fish hatchery lies on the right, just west of the junction of VT 107 and VT 12.

As the valley widens, the river also becomes wider and fans out over a series of gravel bars. The Third Branch enters from the left just above the VT 107/12 bridge at Bethel. An excellent access lies on the right upstream of the bridge (mi. 25¾).

Bethel to Sharon (11¾ miles)

The river below Bethel can be run in a fairly wet summer, but in drier weather the riffles over the gravel bars require some wading. On a warm day this is not at all unpleasant.

Wherever the White makes a sharp left turn the rock configuration causes the water to be deeper, faster, and rougher on the outside (right side) of the curve. Therefore, in low water you should keep to the right for the deeper channels, and in high water keep to the left for channels not runnable in lower water. Where the river curves to the right, no particular patterns prevail.

To begin a trip at Bethel, put in on the right above the VT 107/12 bridge. One mile from the Bethel bridge a fast drop lies immediately below the site of an old power dam (mi. 26¾).

From here the 10-mile run to Sharon is generally easy in medium water, with frequent riffles and occasional class 1 to 2 ledges. The road follows the river, and many places offer access. Just below the high I-89 bridge (mi. 28½), a side road on the left comes close and offers access to the river. The Second Branch enters from the left just above the North Royalton bridge (mi. 29½), and in another 1¾ miles you reach the small town of Royalton (mi. 31¼). One-half mile farther downstream a railroad bridge crosses the river over a small island. About 1 mile below the island a large rock ledge juts out from the left shore just below a transverse ledge. Most people look this over before running it. A big rocky ledge with a huge pool below, it makes a delightful spot to land for a picnic and swim.

This ledge and all other difficult spots from here down to Hartford, except for an old dam below Sharon, can be easily scouted in advance from VT 14. However, a strong class 2 party may not need to look these over again before running them.

The First Branch drains into the White River at South Royalton (mi. 33), which is in fact northeast of Royalton. The ledge just below the bridge here is best scouted in advance from the bridge. Another mile brings you to a small group of sandy islands whose shorelines change with each storm.

Just above Sharon, I-89 recrosses the river (mi. 36¾). The best take-out here is by a Quonset hut on the left bank between I-89 and the Sharon bridge (mi. 37½).

Sharon to West Hartford (6¼ miles)

From Sharon to West Hartford ledges similar to those you have already passed occur with greater frequency. The most difficult spot from Bethel to Hartford lies 1¾ miles below the Sharon bridge, where the river swings right and VT 14 climbs high on the left. High abutments on each bank indicate where an old dam lies at the foot of the mountain notch here (mi. 39¼). In medium water the dam is best run on the right or lined or carried on the left. The hydraulic is strong enough to trap a canoe. Although this dam is difficult to scout in advance, a dirt track off VT 14 at the southern end of the mountain does lead partway to the dam. The river and the road meet again near a railroad bridge ½ mile below; put in here if you wish to avoid the dam.

The ledges over the next 4 miles to West Hartford provide an enjoyable class 2 run at medium water, with drops and high waves alternating with smoother sections. Many places have a fair current and waves, but no rocks and a good run-out, and offer excellent opportunities to practice canoe rescues and swimming in rapids.

The large island ½ mile above West Hartford (mi. 43¾) has a 3-foot ledge on the left that requires a fair amount of water to run. The drop on

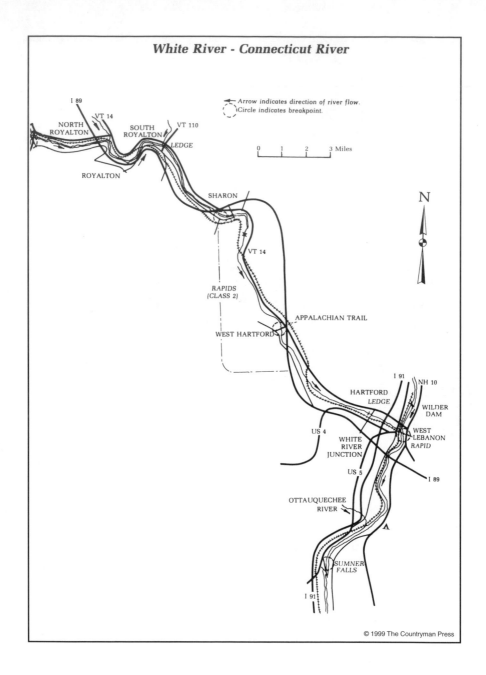

White River - Connecticut River

Arrow indicates direction of river flow.
Circle indicates breakpoint.

I 89
VT 14
NORTH
ROYALTON
SOUTH
ROYALTON
VT 110
LEDGE
ROYALTON

0   1   2   3 Miles

N

SHARON

VT 14

RAPIDS
(CLASS 2)

APPALACHIAN TRAIL

WEST HARTFORD

I 91
NH 10

HARTFORD
LEDGE
WILDER
DAM

US 4
WHITE
RIVER
JUNCTION
WEST
LEBANON
RAPID

US 5
I 89

OTTAUQUECHEE
RIVER
A

SUMNER
FALLS

I 91

© 1999 The Countryman Press

the right, where the river breaks into three channels around a sweeping curve, is more gradual.

West Hartford to Connecticut River (7¼ miles)

The West Hartford bridge (mi. 43¾), crossed by the Appalachian Trail, marks the end of the White's most exciting rapids and many canoe groups take out here.

The remaining 7¼ miles to the Connecticut River, however, do contain some riffles and ledges and offer a good quickwater run. The ledges in this section are sharper on canoe bottoms than the smoother ones above. A fast current brings you to a big ledge just above the Hartford bridge (mi. 49½), where another possible take-out is upstream on the right bank. It is another 1½ miles through the city of White River Junction and under several bridges to the Connecticut River (mi. 51).

Connecticut River

White River to Sumner Falls (7¾ miles)

The run on the Connecticut River to the take-out above Sumner Falls (also called the Hartland Rapid) offers an additional 7¾ miles with only two short runnable drops that kick up some waves. However, water levels can fluctuate wildly and suddenly along this stretch; this depends on the power requirements of the Wilder Dam electrical generating plant, 2 miles north of White River Junction. (A visitors information center is at the New Hampshire end of the dam.)

The I-89 bridge crosses high overhead 1¼ miles below the confluence, and ½ mile beyond a small island marks the first easy drop. Another mile of paddling bring you to the Burnap's Island Campsite (#10, mi. 54), access is from the west side. Just below is the mouth of the Ottauquechee River (mi. 56¼) on the right, and shortly after more high waves at the second drop.

Watch for a large rock in the middle of the river 2 miles below the second drop. This rock, which poses no problem itself, signals that you are approaching the dangerous Sumner Falls. A warning sign is sometimes posted on the Vermont side. After a sweeping curve to the left, rocky ledges appear on the right shore and in the middle of the river.

Take out on the right above the rock outcropping (mi. 58¾), where a sign should mark the portage. Although the first rapids look trivial, each successive drop gets worse, culminating in a series of falls that lie out of view beyond the far island.

In high water the river thunders impressively over the falls, while in low water the bared ledges reveal a series of interestingly scoured potholes. If you walk out to inspect the potholes, be extremely careful: The ledges are worn smooth and coated with silt and mud. Remember also that a head of water released from Wilder Dam can sweep down the river without warning. You can easily launch a canoe below the falls for sight-seeing.

The recommended take-out at the outcropping leads to a parking area that can be reached by car from US 5. At 3.2 miles south of the Ottauquechee River bridge and just north of an I-91 and railroad overpass, take a gravel road to the east leading steeply ¼ mile down to the river. Avoid the obvious paved road leading uphill just to the south between it and the overpass.

~ 15 ~

Lake Champlain

A water trail is being worked out along Lake Champlain, with campsites on both the Vermont and New York shores. This will embody existing state parks, private sites, and primitive sites. Final plans were not available at the time this book went to press. Information and a guidebook may be obtained from:

> Lake Champlain Paddlers' Trail
> 14 South Williams Street
> Burlington, VT 05401
> 802-658-1414
> email: lccchamp@together.net

I made a sample trip to Law Island, recently purchased by the state of Vermont, where primitive camping is allowed. Previously I had paddled the length of Lake Champlain on a Green Mountain Club trip. The leader had researched wind direction, and determined the wind was from the south three days out of five in June, so we paddled south to north, which proved to be correct.

On this occasion in August, there was a brisk wind from the northwest as we paddled north. The following day, when we returned south, the wind was much stronger and from the southwest. Rounding an exposed point was difficult because we were paddling against 3-foot waves. Had I been with a less strong and skillful partner, this would have been impossible. Check weather reports in advance carefully. If you are not camped at a location with car access and your car present, be sure to have an alternate plan available in case the forecast is wrong or you have other problems.

The lake is heavily traveled by boats of all sizes and kinds. This can create considerable problems in the narrow southern section on a weekend.

Lake Champlain, near the mouth of Otter Creek, looking north; the cliffs on the New York side are on the left.

Farther north, where the lake is miles wide, the boats are generally considerate; still, the lake is usually rough.

A major trip on Lake Champlain is only for strong and confident paddlers, but it is a wonderful experience. The water is clear and inviting, and the nearby shores and distant mountain scenery are outstanding. Paddlers seeking an easier and safer trip can enjoy the bays, rocky shores, and beaches.

Let Backcountry Guides Take You There

Our experienced backcountry authors will lead you to the finest trails, parks, and back roads in the following areas:

50 Hikes Series
50 Hikes in the Adirondacks
50 Hikes in Connecticut
50 Hikes in the Maine Mountains
50 Hikes in Coastal and Southern Maine
50 Hikes in Massachusetts
50 Hikes in Maryland
50 Hikes in Michigan
50 Hikes in the White Mountains
50 More Hikes in New Hampshire
50 Hikes in New Jersey
50 Hikes in Central New York
50 Hikes in Western New York
50 Hikes in the Mountains of North Carolina
50 Hikes in Ohio
50 Hikes in Eastern Pennsylvania
50 Hikes in Central Pennsylvania
50 Hikes in Western Pennsylvania
50 Hikes in the Tennessee Mountains
50 Hikes in Vermont
50 Hikes in Northern Virginia

Walks and Rambles Series
Walks and Rambles on Cape Cod and the Islands
Walks and Rambles on the Delmarva Peninsula
Walks and Rambles in the Western Hudson Valley
Walks and Rambles on Long Island
Walks and Rambles in Ohio's Western Reserve
Walks and Rambles in Rhode Island
Walks and Rambles in and around St. Louis

25 Bicycle Tours Series
25 Bicycle Tours in the Adirondacks
25 Bicycle Tours on Delmarva
25 Bicycle Tours in Savannah and the Carolina Low Country
25 Bicycle Tours in Maine
25 Bicycle Tours in Maryland
25 Bicycle Tours in the Twin Cities and Southeastern Minnesota
30 Bicycle Tours in New Jersey
30 Bicycle Tours in the Finger Lakes Region
25 Bicycle Tours in the Hudson Valley
25 Bicycle Tours in Ohio's Western Reserve
25 Bicycle Tours in the Texas Hill Country and West Texas
25 Bicycle Tours in Vermont
25 Bicycle Tours in and around Washington, D.C.
30 Bicycle Tours in Wisconsin
25 Mountain Bike Tours in the Adirondacks
25 Mountain Bike Tours in the Hudson Valley
25 Mountain Bike Tours in Massachusetts
25 Mountain Bike Tours in New Jersey
Backroad Bicycling in Connecticut
Backroad Bicycling on Cape Cod, Martha's Vineyard, and Nantucket
Backroad Bicycling in Eastern Pennsylvania
The Mountain Biker's Guide to Ski Resorts

Bicycling America's National Parks Series
Bicycling America's National Parks: Arizona & New Mexico
Bicycling America's National Parks: California
Bicycling America's National Parks: Oregon & Washington
Bicycling America's National Parks: Utah & Colorado

We offer many more books on hiking, fly-fishing, travel, nature, and other subjects. Our books are available at bookstores and outdoor stores everywhere. For more information or a free catalog, please call 1-800-245-4151 or write to us at The Countryman Press, P.O. Box 748, Woodstock, Vermont 05091. You can find us on the Internet www.countrymanpress.com.